BALLYBUNION

BALLYBUNION

AN ILLUSTRATED HISTORY

DANNY HOULIHAN

The
History
Press

Ballybunion: An Illustrated History
is dedicated to all the people, past and present, who love and loved the traditional seaside town of Ballybunion.

First published 2011
Reprinted 2024

The History Press
97 St George's Place,
Cheltenham, Gloucestershire GL5 3QB

www.thehistorypress.co.uk
© Danny Houlihan, 2011

British Library Cataloguing in Publication Data.
A catalogue record for this book is available from the British Library.

ISBN 978 1 84588 999 9

Typesetting and origination by The History Press
Printed by TJ Books Limited, Padstow, Cornwall

MIX
Paper | Supporting
responsible forestry
FSC® C013056
FSC
www.fsc.org

Contents

Acknowledgements

The author wishes to thank all those who have contributed to *Ballybunion: An Illustrated History*, with both photographic and historical information, and those who gave freely of their time in the last twenty-two years: without their valued help this publication would not have been possible.

The author wishes to thank the following people: Robert (Bobby) O'Mahony, Master, Rathavanigh National School; John Higginbotham; John J. O'Carroll; Shane and Christina Tydings, Tralee; Angela Gilmore, historian; Thomas Walsh, Baranadarrig; Jim McMahon, Ballybunion; Ger Kennelly; Thomas J. O'Donoghue, Glin; Paul and Julie O'Donoghue, photographer, Ballylongford; Patrick Donegan, Hazzelblad photographer, Causeway; Frank O'Connor, Ballybunion; Michael Flahive, maritime historian; Dr Michael Mauson, geological adviser, Duram University; Patrick Fitzgibbon, Listowel; Patsy Costello, golf; Carmel McCarron; T.J. McCarron, coastguard; Liam Mulvihill; Tim Hannon; Padraigh O'Sullivan; Professor Vandyke, Cork University; John Dee, Ballylongford; The Lawrence Collection, National Library Dublin; Joanne Kelly Walsh; and Sean Quinlan, *The Great Book of Kerry*.

Thanks also to those who contributed to this book and research and who are not with us anymore: the late Kit Ahern; Gerard O'Connor; Joe Hillard, Listowel; Chris Hellard, Exchange; Tim Horgan, Farranstack; James Fitzgerald, Pipe Major; Mary Noonan; Matt O'Sullivan; Tim Lyons and James Francis Lyons; Mickey Joe O'Connor; Patsy Fogarty, Doon and Moohane; Jack Walsh, local historian; Matty Leahy, Bromore historian; Phil Clarke, historian, and Phyllis Diggins, Church Road.

The author would like to thank anyone who helped in the production of this work.

The author has endeavoured to credit all historical sources who have contributed both history, photographs and sourced information for this publication. If any source has been omitted these sources will be given due credit in future reprints and publications.

Introduction

The beautiful seaside town of Ballybunion has for centuries welcomed visitors from all over the world; its two golden sandy beaches afford the bather time to swim and relax, and for those of a sporting nature two championship golf courses are located in the resort.

Natural formations such as sea stacks and sea arches adorn the coast, as wild porpus and dolphin swim in the unpolluted waters off the Ballybunion coastline. The rocks in the area are of great interest to mineralogists and geologists, and the cliffs are alive with sea birds, a bird watcher's dream. The town of Ballybunion has what any visitor wants, variety in modern times, the hallmark of quality.

Looking back through the mists of time, Ballybunion has had a fascinating history, from its shore-dweller arrivals along its coastline, through the Bronze Age, Iron Age, early Christian and medieval periods, to the Great Famine and the lost generation. Also of significant interest are its remarkable maritime history and the quest to develop one of the country's finest seaside towns.

Ballybunion: An Illustrated History takes the reader on a journey through Ballybunion's rich heritage and culture, highlighting aspects of its long forgotten history.

Danny Houlihan, September 2010

Ballybunion from the Stone Age to the Vikings

HUNTER-GATHERERS OF BALLYBUNION

Introduction to the Period

The Mesolithic period takes its name from the old stone age and, according to local historians, places the period between the Paleolithic and the Neolithic Stone ages. Geologists who visit the area state that the sea level was lower and the land was covered with a blanket of rich foliage. This period, or epoch, is very important as it signifies the arrival of the first settlers to the shores of Ireland and especially to the area of Ballybunion. The first arrivals and the settlement of these people occurred during a period called the Boreal Phase, when the countryside was covered with a rich blanket of trees such as pines and birch.

Geological surveys in the area suggest that the sea level was much lower than it is today in the Ballybunion and Balleagh area. The animals that roamed were small at that particular time, such as hare and wild pig. The clear flowing rivers such as the Feale, which entered the Cashen, provided a rich catch of fish and marine life, and the unpolluted air was full of birds, which meant that the area was suitable for a settlement, the daily life of which centred on food gathering.

The early tools here were wrought from stone, wood, antler, and most commonly shell. The chief material which was sourced and used in the manufacture of early tools was flint, obtained from the cliff face on the strand of Ballybunion. Veins of this rock can still be seen today and it was extracted by these early settlers in the rock deposits along the Ballybunion coastline using primitive tools.

Settlement Location

The location and orientation of the settlement site was the first aspect that the hunter-gatherer of Ballyeagh–Ballybunion examined. The prime location was the long stretch of naturally formed sand dunes which was located one mile along the coastline to the south of Ballybunion

*Sand dunes of Ballyeagh–
Ballybunion.*

Shell Valley antlers.

Above: *Stone axe.*

Right: *Stone axe, Ballybunion.*

and was rich in native red deer, wild pig and fowl. The area was known as Ballyeagh or Baile an Fhia, 'the townland of the deer'. The high sand dunes concealed the smoke from the ancient fires and gave the settlement protection from the winds. Another factor, and probably the most important in relation to the settlement, was a water source which was sited within the sand dune complex of Ballyeagh. A small stream meanders there to this very day and is known locally as Kitty's River. This area was perfect for a settlement site. Burnt stone, antler fragments and shell deposits have been found near this stream. Indeed many locals have informed the author that a stone hut site existed up to a number of years ago but nothing remains today due to land reclamation. All these elements proved vital to the establishment of a community of early shore dwellers.

Kitchen-Midden Culture of the Sand Hills of Balleagh–Ballybunion

During the 1900s, a number of pioneering field trips were made to the sand hills by antiquarians, in order to find the clues to the coast of Ballybunion. These first excavations unearthed perfect finds of antiquity, such as well-marked hut sites and cooking hearths still preserved within the dune complex, as well as shell middens still covered by the sands of time.

Shell Valley was one of the biggest middens, up to 50ft high and around 200ft wide. Deer antlers, bone comb fragments, shells, limpets and winkles were unearthed at this site, which is now covered by a green on the Cashen golf course. The largest midden on the famous Old Course, Ballybunion, was sited on the hill now known as the Sahara. Here the combination of burnt stone, shells and even human remains such as skulls were uncovered.

The Mystery of the Ballyeagh–Ballybunion Settlement Uncovered

The settlers in the sand dunes lived principally on shellfish which were obtained from the rocks in the nearby strand of Ballybunion. The tools, such as scrappers, which were used to extract the shellfish, were fashioned from stone. Antlers were also used as cutting tools.

The largest settlement site was located midway in the dune complex. A flat area was chosen with a huge sand hill to their backs for protection – this area is still known as 'rabbit warren' or 'rabbit valley', which is sited today just off the old 12th tee box (which is elevated now, and not in use).

In evaluating the settlement the following has been generally accepted: that these pioneering settlers arrived by boat along the coast of Ballybunion, cooked in open fires within the dunes and scattered their refuse in large heaps. Their dwellings were constructed in a temporary manner (allowing them to move on quickly) with the hides from the deer of Ballyeagh covering them. They killed and skinned the native red deer on a rock out in the beach called the Meat Rock, or Caraige Feola, and the sea washed the blood from the freshly killed deer.

Canoe Users

The settlers of Ballyeagh–Ballybunion were, according to local legend, great canoe users and as hunter-gatherers they would have traversed the Cashen basin for wild salmon. Knockanore Hill, the settlement at Ballyeagh–Ballybunion, had ample hunting grounds for venison, a much-needed food supply to supplement the diet of shellfish. When the food chain was used up in the Ballybunion area, the settlers quickly moved to another more bountiful area along the coast.

Artefacts Remaining

Over the years, with heavy rain and sand movement, bones, shells and scrapers have been unearthed. What is certain is that more excavation will be needed in the sand hills of Ballybunion.

BRONZE AGE BALLYBUNION

Fulachtaí Fia: Ancient Cooking Places of Ballybunion

In modern times in the Ballybunion and Beal areas, burnt stone and wooden troughs have been unearthed. These were the ancient outdoor cooking places of ancestors, which were called 'Fulacht Fiadh', or 'the cooking place of the deer'. Fulachtaí Fia can be found in most areas but go unnoticed due to field cover and natural vegetation. In the landscape of Ballybunion all that remains are the horseshoe-shaped mounds which have been uncovered, with heaps of burnt stone scattered around the ancient hearths.

Water Source

During the Bronze Age in the area, the Fulachtaí Fia were located close to water sources. What remains in the Ballybunion area backs this up; back in antiquity these travellers did not want for water.

Construction of Fulachtaí Fia

The trough was made out of a trunk of a tree which was felled in the local area of Ballybunion. The internal part of the trough was hollowed out so as to retain water, and it was then buried to a depth of 2ft below the ground level of the hearth. Here, it could retain the water which would seep in from the damp field or which was put there by hand.

Cooking in the Fulachtaí Fia

Tradition has been handed down in the area that, to cook in the pit, a large fire was located near the trough, large stones were placed in the trough by means of a wooden stick, and, when the hot stones made contact with the water, the pit became hot and could be brought to boiling point. A joint of venison, wrapped in straw which preserved it, was then added. The whole process took about four hours, by which time the meat was ready to consume. Over the years and decades to follow, the constant dropping of stones into the pit created a build-up in the horseshoe-shaped mounds which have been unearthed over the years in the Ballybunion area.

Typical Measurements of the Ballybunion Fulachtaí Fia

When the mound was elevated, the Fulachtaí Fia were found to be up to 56ft in diameter. Across the Fulachtaí Fia, 8 to 10ft wide, the trough, according to locals, was anything up to 4ft deep, and side banks were when built up with stone to a height of 4ft. Over the years in the Ballybunion, Beal and Ballyduff areas, where these ancient structures have been found, all that remains are the stones and the odd trough.

In the spring of 1995, local historian Matty Leahy (RIP) brought me to a place at Lick Castle and identified the location and remains of one such Fulacht Fiadh. The horseshoe-shaped mound was there and there were traces of burnt stone everywhere. The pit was still there and was damp. Unfortunately this pit was on the edge of a cliff nearly eroded and since then it has fallen into the sea, lost forever. Only one stone remains.

Ballybunion and its Bronze Age Cist Burial Tombs

Described by eminent archaeologists as stone-lined or stone-flagged graves, these burial tombs enclosed an area measuring (depending on the cists) approximately 6ft by 3ft. These structures were covered with a capstone or a number of capstones depending on the type of the cists, which came in various sizes. The first type was called a short cist, where the remains were placed in the grave in a cramped position; the knees brought up near the chin and tied with a rope. One could say that the remains were, in some cases, forced into the grave.

The grave uncovered in Sandhill Road, Ballybunion, during the 1980s was of the long cist type, and consisted of a large capstone which was placed on top of upright flagstones, which were laid on either side to box the cist grave. In the area adjacent to the grave, large amounts of soil had been deposited. This was due to the digging of the ceremonial pit and the soil would have later been dispersed and backfilled on the grave. In the Ballybunion area these graves became overgrown with grass; the humps of earth subsided over the centuries into the landscape until modern land reclamation would eventually uncover the graves.

In researching the Ballybunion cist graves, it has emerged that in some cases a ceremonial urn or pot used to store food was found within the confines of the graves, but this was not the case in the cist found at Sandhill Road, Ballybunion. In some cists the urn was used for cremations, but the Ballybunion graves were all full burials and no urns were found. Ballybunion's cist graves contained well-preserved skeletons. Most were orientated eastwards, according to local sources, with the body placed on its side and the head facing east, which obviously has some Celtic connection.

In the 1800s, a number of long cists were uncovered in the sand hills of Ballyeagh by pioneering field expeditions, however not much is known about these graves. On Spraymount Road (now Cliff Road), on the property of Mr Raymond, a number of long stone-lined cists were uncovered.

During the 1980s, while working on the construction of the Marconi Housing, the father of the author, the late Sean Houlihan, uncovered a cist grave with his excavator. Large foundation trenches were being prepared to be filled with Ready Mix, and Sean related that:

Ballybunion cist.

When I struck the bucket of the digger into the ground the excavator met with extreme resistance, in fact it shook the machine. It gave me a fright. A large flat stone was pulled up from the soil and I then jumped out to see what I had uncovered. It was a grave. The head of the skeleton was larger than our own; its teeth were perfect, the bones were brown and it lay with the head faced southwards.

I asked what happened to the grave and the bones, but it seems they were removed quickly and the work was moved on.

What is clear is that these graves were sited in areas where daily movement and traffic occurred. In the Ballybunion area, the location of the sites is very important, as tradition relates that an ancient roadway or highway network connected the area with the famous Cliadh Rua, which ran from Maulin Mountain on Kerry Head. This ancient road ran along the commons of Maulin Mountain, skirted along the coast through Clasmealcon and then crossed the River Cashen by a narrow wooden bridge. The road network ran through the sand dunes of Ballyeagh, along the coast of the present town of Ballybunion to Doon, where it forked towards the summit of Knockanore and from here towards Charleville, connecting with the Cliadh Dubh Na Ratha.

These old roadways are sometimes referred to as toghers or causeways and are mentioned in the history of St Bridget by Cogitous in the seventh century. These ancient structures were just

Cliadh Rua, Knockanore.

Matty Leahy.

wide enough to allow a wooden cart and animals to pass. The toghers were also used in bogs, where they were raised if the area was very damp.

It is fair to state that during the Bronze Age, if a nobleman or a person of high stature died along one of these road networks, they would have been buried in this fashion, thus the cists of Ballybunion are unique. Further excavation and evidence will yield more insight into this aspect of Ballybunion's history.

IRON AGE BALLYBUNION

During the Iron Age, 500 BC–AD 500, our distant ancestors took full advantage of the steep and vertical cliffs that the Ballybunion area provided. Settlers erected large fosse or ditches which divided the neck of the promontory and those inside the settlement lived in relative peace. So well chosen were these ancient fortifications that later in the medieval period, castles, such as Ballybunion, were constructed within the old earthworks.

The Great Promontory Fort of Ballybunion and Doon

The great promontory of Ballybunion, where Ballybunion Castle stands today, is a prime example of our Iron Age past; one can just imagine the great excavations on the site where the castle now stands, the early tools and the local manpower used to cut into the sheer cliff face and to construct dwellings in a relatively dangerous position, perched high, overlooking both sandy beaches in Ballybunion. The high mound which was excavated from the fosse is still there to this day and exhibits the sheer work involved in digging out the fosse, as the earthen bank is at present over 10ft.

About a mile north of Ballybunion on the coastline of Doon is sited the best preserved coastal promontory fort, Lissadooneen, another prime example of our Early Iron Age past. It has a curved fosse and earthworks about 105ft along the fosse and on the approach to the fosse there is a late ditch measuring 27ft, the burial place of a ship's crew. The disaster and the circumstances of their burial are not known, but it was probably the result of a shipwreck, of which there were many in the area.

The entrance to the fort is through a gap in the fosse about 9ft wide and 10ft below the field the inner ring is very steep. At the southern end one can see to this day the stages of construction in the building of Lissadooneen.

Crescent Fort of Doon

The crescent-shaped fort of Doon is quite impressive; in fact one could describe it as the Dun Aengus of Kerry. Large banks and fosse guard this ancient stronghold located in the townland of Doon. This area incorporated a large settlement and also had an elaborate underground network of souterrains, which is preserved to this day. It is rare for forts such as this one to have survived the ravages of time and lasted into the modern era.

The Ring Forts

The ring fort or rath is the most common field monument in the Ballybunion area and many good examples remain, which are protected by the state and the landowners. At one time there were up to 400 raths in the area but over the years this number has diminished to but a few.

These monuments date from the Iron Age, 300 BC-AD 500, and are located in most townlands of the parish, such as Ballybunion, Beale and Killconly. Ring forts in the area measure between 25m to 50m and the majority in the Ballybunion area are of univallate design. Faha, another fort at Doon, is also very well preserved.

The ring forts of the area have another interesting feature – underground chambers called souterrains, meaning 'below land'. Ballybunion has many of these associated with its fort network. However, they are extremely dangerous and should be approached with caution.

The design of ring forts in the Ballybunion area consisted of dry stone walls with large flaggers used as lintels over doors. These structures were elaborately designed to facilitate storage, safety and escape. Ballybunion Castle, Pookeenee Castle and Lick Castle all have examples within their confines.

Souterrain entrance, Ballybunion.

Stonework in the souterrain.

THE EARLY CHRISTIAN PERIOD

The Origins and Development of Kill as a Church Name in the Ballybunion Area

Research has been undertaken into this aspect of Ballybunion's local history in the last forty to fifty years. Many theories have been recorded and research papers written regarding the words 'Kill' or 'Cill' meaning a church or cell unit. What is certain is that in the area of Ballybunion, Kill or Cill is associated with a settlement of Christian or missions which established a base within the North Kerry area from which to spread the Christian message. One large settlement was established around the eighth century by St Senan of Scattery, and North Kerry, Killconly and Killeithne in the Ballybunion area were under its initial control.

In those early days of pre-Christian settlement in the area, the pre-Patrick missions sought out quiet, peaceful glens and islands off the Ballybunion coast and often located their settlements near water sources (Killconly and Killeithne have water sources near their respective sites). In all locations within the Ballybunion area, settlements were constructed near water sources, so clearly these missions were here to stay; that was until the dawn of the year 800, when the tranquil waters of the Shannon estuary were broken with a reign of carnage and destruction for the Christian settlements.

The year 800 saw the arrival of Viking long ships and with them the establishment of one of the biggest Viking long-ship bases on the Shannon estuary. From here the Vikings raided the inland waterways from Scattery Island to Limerick. In the townland of Ballyeagh, at the mouth of the Cashen estuary, an island called Inis Labrinde or Leabhrainn, 'the Island of Books', was first to be attacked by the Vikings. The pre-Patrick settlers had to flee to the woods near Derryco and finally to Rattoo.

The settlements in the Ballybunion area were diverse: one was called Cill Eithne, another Cill Chonnla. The former was established by a holy woman called Eithne and the other by monk called Chonnla, who is said to have established his mission from Scattery Island.

Killeithne or the Church or Cell of St Eithne

South of the present town of Ballybunion is a graveyard which bears the name Killehenny or Killeithne. It is attributed to the woman who established an early mission in the area. It is said that she was a kind and gentle person who took care of people in need. Eithne's patron day was 12 July but it is no longer celebrated here.

Local historians have said that the small church was located within the confines of where the graveyard is now situated and that it was very small in construction. Others believe that the church was burnt and that it was located adjacent to the graveyard in a field directly across from the site. Artefacts such as quern-stones and other items of settlement ware have been found within the graveyard during the digging of old graves, thus suggesting that the settlement was in fact sited where the graveyard is today.

When one looks at the old maps of the ancient Kingdom of Kerry another name in the area of Ballybunion occurs, that of Killconly, the church and cell of St Chonnla.

Scattery Island monastic settlement. (Photo and information courtesy of Mary Noonan RIP)

Iron Age rotary quern stone.

St Eithne's graveyard.

Killconly church.

Archaeologists have rendered a date of the twelfth to thirteenth century for the building of the church. These dates place Killconly at the end of the Early Christian period and the dawn of the medieval period.

The church building measures 13m to 14m in length and it is over 6m wide; the windows were located on the east and south sides and were of long vertical design, measuring 15cm in width. The door on the southern side was constructed with small hammered flagstones which were obtained from the face of the nearby cliffs. To this day the doorway features a round-headed arch.

Tradition relates that one day, as Chonnla was out collecting wild berries, a serpent from a nearby fort called Liss Na Peasna attached him. The monk quickly drew a sword from under his habit and slew the serpent on the hill next to the graveyard, thus lending its name to the church.

Rattoo Monastic Settlement

During the Viking raids at the mouth of the Cashen River around AD 800, the early settlers fled along the riverbanks to avoid bloodshed and on their journey they found the secluded hillside of Rattoo.

In Rattoo there was a fort called Rath Mhaighe Na Tuaiscirt, 'the fort on the north plain', which dated from the Early Christian period. It was during the sixth to seventh centuries that a bishopric was established here under Bishop Lugach, who set up a monastic centre there.

Rattoo Abbey.

Rattoo Round Tower.

The round tower was constructed between the seventh and ninth centuries. This *cloig teach*, or bell house, was built for the sanctuary of the monks in the settlement, who, if attacked by Norse invaders, could find a place of refuge. The uppermost part of the tower, the belfry, housed the famous Rattoo Bell, which rang each day and night during the life of the settlement.

Tradition relates that during one particular Viking raid, the bell was removed by the monks from the round tower and carried along the riverbanks by the abbots to the River Brick, where they cast the bell into the water for eternity.

Around the year 800, from their base on the Island of Scattery, the Vikings plundered up the estuary from Inis Labrinn or Learbhann at the mouth of the Cashen to Derryco and from there to the monastic settlement at Rattoo. Centuries of destruction were to follow.

It is not known when the demise of Rattoo actually occurred, but due to the suppression of the monasteries by the English king, the future of Irish missions was under severe threat. In the year 1200, the Knights Hospitallers of St John took over the settlement and in the decades to follow, the Order of Arrosian Canons took over, and they held the settlement until 1590. In the state papers of 1276 King Edward confirmed Brother Christian as Abbot. Later, in 1336, an abbot at Rattoo was pardoned for harbouring Maurice fitz Nicholas.

Today the round tower, church and abbey are reminders of a great period in church building in the area and a time filled with fear and with Christian beliefs.

MEDIEVAL BALLYBUNION

Ballybunion Castle

Ballybunion Castle, or from the old maps Castle Bale Bonan, was constructed around the dawn of the 1500s by a branch of the Geraldines of West Limerick and was later inhabited by the Fitzmaurices, Lords of Kerry, who resided at Lixnaw. The Geraldine forces passed the castle on to a family called Bonzons or Bunyan and the present town of Ballybunion takes its name from them.

Ballybunion Castle was destroyed by Lord Kerry in 1582 and in 1583 William Og Bunyan had his lands confiscated due to his active role in the Desmond rebellion. Waiting in the wings

Above: *Ballybunion Castle, 1900s.*

Left: *Ballybunion Castle on the eve of the lightning strike.*

Ballybunion Castle today.

was a notorious rebel, Thomas Fitzmaurice, who made a submission to King James and had the lands of Ballybunion confirmed on him by letters patent 1612.

The castle came under the ownership of landlord Richard Hare in 1783 and in the 1900s it passed to the Local Improvements Committee. In the 1960s the castle was sold to Kerry County Council, who now has sole responsibility for the ruin. During the winter of 1998 the castle was struck by lighting and the upper part of the tower was destroyed. Although the sight identified the town for centuries, it has sadly not since been restored.

Ballybunion Castle Construction

The castle was built on a former coastal promontory fort of the Clann O'Connor; the cut stone for the castle was quarried locally and brought by horse to the site by slaves in military perpetuity. The castle was a tower house in design, was four storeys high and was vaulted. Ballybunion Castle has a spiral staircase which winds in an anti-clockwise direction, which is unique in this area.

Access to the roof and the battlements were by wooden stairs. The basement was large, to accommodate supplies, and the exterior pointing on the walls was of a lime mortar and ox blood mix. The roof was either slate or thatch, as both materials were available in the area.

Underground Passages

The castle also tapped into the underground souterrain network laid down during the Iron Age settlement and used the structure for storage and for strategic planning. In the 1800s the local parish priest Fr Mortimer O'Connor discovered more souterrains and ordered them to be filled in on the ladies' beach side of the castle.

Today the ruin of Ballybunion Castle stands proudly on the cliff top, bearing testament to the workers who built it and the Bunyans who gave us our proud name, Ballybunion.

Above: *Ballybunion Castle, western side.*

Left: *Spiral stairs, Ballybunion Castle.*

Above: *Ballybunion Castle and strand, 1900s.*

Right: *Unglazed window, Ballybunion Castle.*

Lick Castle, 1300s

The ruin of the once grand tower house Leac Beibhionn guards the western promontory of Faha, in the old civil parish of Killconly. Lick Castle takes its name from Caislean Leac Beibhionn, 'the Castle of the Fair-Haired Woman'. In the maps of the sixteenth century the castle is called Lickbevune.

Lick Castle, which was one of the first tower houses in the area, was built at the end of the 1300s and beginning of the 1400s by the Clann Richard of Leac Beibhionn. This clann took their lineage from Richard, the second son of Maurice, sixth Baron of Kerry.

In *The Annals of The Kingdom of Ireland by the Four Masters* we read of a turbulent history of Lick Castle, a history steeped in the blood of its masters and lords. In 1568, James, son of

Lick Castle, 1900s.

Maurice Fitzgerald, marched with a number of others against Thomas, Lord Kerry, on behalf of the Geraldines. James and his company besieged Mac Maurice at in Lixnaw Castle, but the attackers were unprepared and were crushed, leaving among their slain Jon, son of Garret Fitzgerald, the heir to Leac Beibhionn.

In 1582 we read of more atrocities by Mac Maurice; he destroyed Listowel, Lixnaw, Beale, Ballybunion and Lick Castles, leaving the last of these without a master. The annals state that Mac Maurice retreated to the woods, but it was not long before Captain Zouch entered the area in search of Mac Maurice and traversed the woods. Lick Castle was at that time barren and without a master, but Captain Zouch reinstated the master and its inhabitants.

Lick Castle was then ruled by its lawful owners for some time. In the centuries to come, the Clann Richard of Leac Bheibhionn was to lose their lands and in the 1600s the castle was destroyed and its demesne granted to Trinity College Dublin.

Leac Bheibhionn Construction and Ruin

In various historical sources the castle was described as a peel tower and had a height of 70ft and a length of 30ft. However, it is next to impossible to gauge its total dimensions as erosion has eaten away the ruin. The tower rose on the edge of a cliff on the east corner and had a window facing south. The castle, according to local historian Matty Leahy, was four storeys high and was vaulted to facilitate storage and a secret passageway. The window recesses were 3ft thick and the west wall 4ft thick; the east wall was 8ft and the southern wall 6ft 10in.

The author surveyed the castle with the late Matty Leahy during the late 1980s and according to Matty, Lick Castle had a basement that years ago could be entered by means of an opening at low tide. We could not see the entrance because the chasm was choked by wall debris from the castle above. Access to Lick Castle was by means of a drawbridge, although its exact location has now vanished due to erosion. On the site we noticed that the west walls had very small window openings and Matty pointed out that a water source was at one time located on the island by means of a spring well, now covered. A cutting in the rocks for small boats is still located in the area.

Over the years, lead shot has been found in the rocks near Lick Castle, which was used by the advancing forces of Mac Maurice as they besieged the castle. This lead shot was used by locals over the centuries as weights for fishing.

The Clann Richard had their own currency on the promontory, one local person informed the author that they found an oddly shaped coin with writing inscribed on it, which they surmised was probably used as currency. The castle had a reputation in the area as being the dampest castle in the country and that during wet periods the walls dripped with damp. This is highly probable due to the castle's location so close to the coast.

Today the ruins of Lick Castle stand testament to the great Clann of Leac Bheibhionn.

Pookeenee Castle

Pookeenee Castle is located on the cliff-path walk between Scolt Na Dhrida and the Nine Daughters Hole. This structure was constructed probably during the reign of Mary Queen of Scots, as in that period double-ditch structures and upper wooden defenses were common. Pookeenee is translated from the Irish as 'the hood of the broken vault'; indeed the vault can still be seen, slightly damaged.

Pookeenee Castle.

Pookeenee Castle vault.

A doorway is still in position, with a round-headed arch. Pookeenee has two narrow windows which face seawards and internal storage vaults are located on both walls and are in good condition. The exterior walls are now suffering from the severe weather, due to the long wet winters and dry summers.

The castle stood on a site with a water source, and was built convex to the land. The castle was an unusual structure in the area and no records remain as who built it, but what is certain is that the nature of its construction was defensive. Locally it is called the jail, in connection with the legends of the area.

THE KINGS WHO RULED FROM DOON

It was said by the old people in the area of Doon Point that the O'Connors built a castle on the promontory overlooking the sea near Ri Na File, 'King of the Cliffs'. Others state that it was an O'Sullivan castle, but the more probable theory would be the former, as we read that Conocubhair ruled from around 966 from his stronghold at Doon.

Tradition relates that Ciar, the son of Queen Meabh of Connacht and Feargus Mor Mac Ri of Ulster, came to this area around AD 75 and was accepted with his warriors as the sept which for centuries ruled the ancient Kingdom of Kerry (or Ciarraighe) from their stronghold on the high cliffs guarding the townland of Doon. In the centuries to follow the sept was known as Concur or Ua Chonocuhuir and they constructed their castle, Doon Castle, on the site of one of their former forts.

Today all that remains of that once grand structure is a few masonry stones covered with grass on the edge of an eroding cliff. In the annals we can get a picture of the area at that time; a time of chieftains, clann warfare and civil unrest. It is not surprising that the Great O'Connor saw his chance to fight when, around the year 800, Vikings attacked the island of Inis Labrinde at the mouth of the Cashen River. It is said that O'Connor gave protection to these settlements along the coast.

Badan Ua Concur was another chief from Doon Point and it is said he attained great stature as leader of his army, called the Carriage Luarchaire, which took part with High King Brian Boru's army which defeated the Viking power on the banks of the Tolka River on Good Friday, 10 April 1014.

Doon Point.

TOWNLANDS AND THEIR LOCAL NAMES

The old civil parish of Ballybunion contained thirteen bailes or, to use the anglicised term, townlands. These townlands had their own divisional land markers and boundaries.

Ahima: A ford or crossing point. Many people in the area have informed the author that there was a ford or crossing in the area but due to land reclamation its exact location cannot be found.

Ballybunion: Bally or Baile means townland or land unit, Bhuinneanaigh derives from the Bunyan or Bonzon family, retainers for the castle. While another name has been suggested – Baile Bun an Anmnach, 'the town at the mouth of the river' – the former seems more likely.

Baile An Fhia or Ballyeagh: The townland of the deer, so named after the abundance of wild red deer in the nearby woods of Knockanore.

Bearnadarrig: The Red Gap.

Dun or Doon: Stronghold or fortified enclosure. The seat of the O'Connor clan around 966.

Fearann Phiarais or Farran Pierce: Pierce's Land.

A view of Ballybunion's townlands.

Gort Na Sceiche or Gort Na Skia: The battle of the shields, or the battle of the ditches or hedges. Associated with the O'Connor history in the area.

Cill Eithne/Cill Athinna or Killehenny: The church or cell of Eithne. According to legend, Eithne was a holy woman who was in the area in the time of St Senan of Scattery. Her small church was apparently sited within the graveyard now called Killehenny.

Leat Ardan or Lahardan: Half a height or platform/plateau. This area rises gradually towards the height at Knockanore and thus takes its name from the rise to the hill.

Mucan or Moohane: Underground passage or smoky hovel.

Rath Oonagh or Rathoonagh: The fort of the grave. One story I was told was that a wise man or druid was buried within the fort along the banks of the Cashen and so the fort took this name.

Dromin: Ridge or height. The townland inclines towards the rise to Knockanore Hill.

Townlands in the old civil parish of Killconly

Acrai: Acres.

Beale or Beal: Mouth, in this case the estuary or mouth of the River Shannon.

Bruach Mor or Bromore: Height of a cliff or height of a hillside.

Ceathru An Caislean or Castle Quarters: The quarters of the castle associated with Beal Castle and its history.

Doire: Oak wood. I have been told that there was a belt of oak trees from beyond Beal to Carrigafoyle in bygone times.

Droim or Drom: Ridge.

Faiche or Faha: The lawn or playing field, named in association with Lick Castle.

Killconly or Cill Chonnla: The church or cell of Chonnla.

Rathavanig: Fort of the monk or small monks' settlement.

Ballybunion in Myth and Legend

THE BATTLE OF CATH CNOC AN FHOMHAIR

This story tells the tale of the heroic attempt by a Grecian princess called Niamh to flee from her native Greece and from the man she once loved. This man was Tailc Mhic Troen, a noted Grecian warrior and sailor whose life had been transformed by an enchantment, wherein his body was transformed into a beast with the head and tail of a cat. Niamh, not wanting to go through with the marriage, fled Greece by boat and eventually ended up in the Atlantic. Many days later, tired and frightened, she landed her ship on the golden beach at Ballybunion.

Strategically located on the headland of Doon, Fionn Mac Cumhaill spotted the lone ship and he proceeded to the strand, where he offered his protection to the fair Niamh, right down to the last warrior in the Fianna.

One week later, the Shannon estuary darkened with the shadow of Tailc's warships. Immediately on landing, Tailc sent his spies into the woods of Knockanore to seek out Niamh. On discovering where his loved one was, he sought revenge. Tradition relates that Tailc, using

The strand where Tailc's warships landed.

The Cat's Hole where Tailc burrowed to the summit of Knockanore.

his cat features, burrowed a hole in the side of the Castle Green and from there he tunnelled to the summit of Knockanore, where he emerged. Once on the summit, Tailc began to slaughter the Fianna in their hundreds. The Fianna, brandishing broadswords, engaged the mighty Tailc and the battle was a fierce one.

The combat went on for days, according to the legend, leaving thousands dead on the summit of Knockanore, until Oscar, son of Fionn, took on the mighty Tailc. With one swift blow, he caught Tailc off guard and Oscar thrust his sword into his groin. As Tailc's life ebbed away, he transformed back into the handsome warrior he once was. On observing this, Niamh felt sorry, took one sigh and died.

THE LOST ISLAND OF KILLSTIFFIN OR KILLSAHEEN

The myths and legends of the Ballybunion and Beale areas include one tale of an island which is said to appear every hundred years in the Shannon estuary. Some said that the island off the coast was small in proportion and appeared with a steeple, houses, people and a typical fair day in progress. Older people from the area have related to me that during certain and rare weather conditions, what was seen on the estuary from Loop Head inwards beyond Killcredan was an atmospheric image fair day on the estuary. However, in one version it was noted that on seeing the island, one would die within a year.

The word Kill (or Cill) refers to a cell or a church structure of some kind, whether primitive or otherwise. During the Early Christian period, the missions sought out the sanctuary of the secluded islands off our coast. These sheltered locations were well chosen for isolation from the greater world and gave them peace to pray.

Stiffin or Stephan is associated with the Kill or Cill in the area, which was a small hermitage or large settlement. We also know that a settlement existed on the Clare side called Cill Credan, but historians are unsure as to who followed whom. Along the estuary there were many early missions and holy men and holy women.

On a low water mark on the estuary each year, a wave breaks out from Killcredan on an underwater bank called the Stiffin Bank, which is marked quite clearly on the Ordnance

The lost island of Killstiffin.

Survey map. Could this be the lost island of the estuary? Only through more underwater investigation will the truth be known. Regardless, this area will always fascinate the historians and people of the locality.

SCOLT NA DHRIDA

Scolt Na Dhrida, or the Druids' Layer, is located on the cliff-path walk north of the town, overlooking a sheer drop to the rocks below. This area, with its views of County Clare in the distance, is steeped in lore and legend.

During the turbulent epoch of the Druids, sacrificial worship to the Celtic gods was seemingly practised in the area and tradition relates that on a May morning, as the dawn broke, a sacrifice in honour of the Celtic god Belelnos was offered. The chosen sacrifice was placed at the abyss near the Scolt facing the Shannon estuary. The ritual was carried out by chosen executioners who began by delivering blows to the victim's head in turn. A garrotte was used to finalise the rite and the body was cast over the cliffs to the raging tide below, concluding the ceremony.

This story is just one of many which have been heard in the area. Today the area is quiet, as visitors enjoy the peaceful walk along the cliffs, unaware of the history behind the name Scolt Na Dhrida.

The Druids' Layer.

The Virgin's Rock.

THE VIRGIN'S ROCK

Rising majestically from the Bay of Doon stands the most photographed naturally formed arch of North Kerry. Home to hundreds of sea birds on an annual basis, at its base dolphins and wild porpus swim unhindered an area of extreme beauty.

In myth and legend the area is associated with the Seagur, a warrior seafarer of the O'Connor Clann, who used the high pinnacle of the Virgin's Rock as his lookout for any Viking long ships that may enter the landscape of Ciar.

One story was that on a particularly fine clear day, as the Seagur was fishing for bass on the rock, a boat containing three Viking scouts came onto the Nun's Strand. Quickly the Seagur climbed down from his lofty perch and engaged the Vikings with all his strength, beheading two and badly injuring the other – a feat worthy of the respect of his chief.

In the Ballybunion area today the Virgin's Rock is well identified with the coastline heritage of Doon and it has been printed on postcards for close to 100 years.

THE NINE DAUGHTERS HOLE SAGA

This tale is set in the pre-medieval period of Ballybunion's history, a time of rival clanns vying for supreme power over their lands. In the Ballybunion area, the ruling clann was the

O'Connor or Ui Choncubhair. The O'Connor clann ruled their lands with marriage alliances and battle forays into the lands of other clanns.

The ruler or king was a fierce chieftain called The O'Connor or Concur, who boasted that he never drank water, only wine. Like most of Ireland's chieftains, he had the pick of the clanswomen as wives and he enjoyed the rich fruits of his reign.

During a respite in clann battles, O'Connor had nine daughters, each one more attractive than the other, who grew up in relative peace at their castle at Doon Point. But relative peace was shattered when, around the year AD 800, a fleet of Viking long ships entered the Cashen estuary, attacking the monastic settlements of Inislabrinde and Derryco.

O'Connor, fearing the loss of his ancestral lands, organised his warriors into battle readiness, and facing his sworn enemy he raised his shield and signalled his mighty army to attack. Sword clashed with sword from high tide to low tide. As the battle raged, war cries filled the tranquil air and the sound of swords clashing was heard up to a mile distant.

The outcome was victory for O'Connor, and nine Viking leaders were captured during the battle. They were tortured and imprisoned at Pookeenee Castle. Many days later, O'Connor's daughters were out in the vicinity of the castle and on seeing the nine specimens of Viking manhood they fell in love and planned to elope. However, O'Connor had a spy in the area who reported these developments back to him. O'Connor immediately plotted his evil revenge.

The chief summoned his nine daughters to the pit now known as the Nine Daughters Hole and told them that his gold torc had fallen in. One by one, each daughter went down the hole in search of the missing treasure, but none came out. O'Connor, being a fair chief, had all nine Viking leaders beheaded and had their bodies cast into the pit along with his daughters.

The Nine
Daughters Hole.

Ballybunion in the Eighteenth and Nineteenth Centuries

A VOLCANO ERUPTS IN BALLYBUNION, 1783

In 1733, along the grassy cliffs of Doon, large sections of cliff face collapsed, causing the minerals in the rocks to ignite, resulting in a large plume of smoke which was seen for miles around. The smoke covered an area from the Ri Na File to Lick Castle and locals in the area were quick to call it a volcano, a story which spread far and wide in those poor times. Donkeys and carts were used to get to the spot, as the tale spread countrywide.

In the Ballybunion village, the local gossips were in their element, adding to the tale. The devil, the banshee and other underworld gods were used in explanations relayed to the visitors, who found the whole escapade very humorous and entertaining.

The eruption caused so much of a commotion that in 1733, Charles Smith, in his history of Kerry, wrote about the volcano, 'Nearly two years ago, a piece of these high cliffs fell off, where upon there broke out a smoke attended with a strong sulphuric smell.' Smith goes on to state that the burning of the cliff face lasted for up to two years and 'wasted away so much of the

Volcano Cliffs, Ballybunion.

cliff that has fallen that a large opening up to 60ft in breath and 100ft in length can be seen'. According to Smith, the local people in the area said it reminded them of a lime kiln, the heat and the smell was so strong. Smith also states that it was humorous to see the way the cliff was burnt and to observe all the colours in the rock strata which had been highlighted during the supposed volcanic eruption.

In the years that followed, the smoke from the cliff face in Doon halted. All the local tales ceased to but a memory and a mention on faded newspapers of the time.

THE BALLYEAGH FACTION FIGHT, 1834

On St John's Day, 24 June 1834, on the golden strand of Ballyeagh, the greatest faction fight of Kerry's history took place. It is written in the annals that 1,200 Cooleens, a faction from the Clannmaurice side of the Cashen estuary, crossed the river by a wooden footbridge to engage in mortal combat with their sworn enemies, the Lawlor Black Mulvihills, who hailed from the Iraghticonner side of the Cashen.

On that famous day, the Lawlor Black Mulvihill faction was gathering in the deep sandhills, where the present Ballybunion Golf Club is located. Battle tactics and plans were finalised, large amounts of poitín were consumed, and weapons such as blackthorn sticks, hurleys, stones and any projectiles which could be employed as weapons were issued to this faction, which numbered 2,000 strong.

As the time approached two o'clock, the military of the 69th regiment under Captain Hooper were strategically positioned just a short distance from the strand on a dune not far from the race site. In the interim, Captain Hooper had succeeded in arresting some of the Lawlor Black Mulvihills faction who were drunk near the hawkers' tents. These tents were set up on the annual race day along the banks of the Cashen, where locals would sell their produce.

It is said locally that after the first race the Cooleens marched from their camp on the Cashen side, crossed the river by the wooden bridge and emerged on the south side of the strand wielding sticks and weapons of all descriptions. The Cooleens were now ready to fight. According to sources, local priest Fr Darby O'Mahony, PP Listowel, pleaded with the faction to 'For God's sake listen to sense', but this call fell on deaf ears.

Captain Hooper, now realising he had a potential riot on his hands, ordered his 69th regiment to line across the strand. This action proved useless, as the sheer numbers overwhelmed the regiment and left them looking very isolated on the strand.

The mighty Cooleens advanced their faction and struck the Lawlor Black Mulvihill faction, who were off guard. The cries ands shrieks of the wounded filled the tranquil air of the Cashen, as the Cooleens and their blackthorn sticks took effect. The Cooleens now had the advantage.

A ragging counterattack was issued from the Lawlor Black Mulvihills, who dropped their poitín jars in the sandhills and forced their way onto the strand of Ballyeagh. Two thousand men, women and old men, armed with blackthorn sticks, cudgels, maces, horseshoes and stones, hacked and slaughtered the Cooleens, who were forced to give ground at four o'clock.

The tide was now on the way out and the Cooleens, realising their cause was lost, ran for their boats with the Lawlor Black Mulvihills in hot pursuit. Along the shoreline the Lawlor

An original blackthorn from Ballyeagh faction fight.

Black Mulvihill faction was amassed, armed with stones and waiting for the moment for when the Cooleens would go for their boats. This moment had arrived and a bombardment of stones and rocks hailed onto the Cooleens as they retreated to the water to such an extent that the boats capsized and the occupants drowned. This was later to known as the 'boat upset'.

Captain Hooper then entered the fight with the 69th regiment and began dispersing the remaining factions, who were still fighting up to the last, even the women. It is said in the Ballybunion area that the strand of Ballyeagh was covered with wounded and dead after that fateful day and that the river was red in colour.

Sworn Inquiry by the English Parliament

The Ballyeagh Fight was so known internationally that many inquiries were undertaken as to what had happened in that little part of Ireland. The English Prime Minister, Lord Melbourne, ordered a sworn inquiry and the results showed on that fateful day on the strand of Ballyeagh, the military of the 69th regiment under Captain Hooper were outnumbered badly, with only sixty rank and file, two subalterns and three NCOs. The cause of the fight was not ascertained but some locals and historians have said, 'They fought for the sheer love of fighting.'

The annual race meeting was banned forever in the area and was moved to Listowel, which now holds the Listowel Race Week each year. Thousands of people still make the journey to stay in Ballybunion during the race week, not realising that the races originated here.

THE GREAT FAMINE IN BALLYBUNION

In recent years, many studies of the Great Famine of 1845-1849 have been undertaken. In some communities there has been reluctance, even to this day, to speak or debate what happened, and Ballybunion is no exception. When we were taught history at school it was a subject often passed over, forgotten. Indeed we may say that we have forgotten the people who died and those who were forced to leave due to starvation and emigration. This brief account paints a picture of Ballybunion during those poor times.

Prior to the Great Famine, there were indicators that something was not right in Ballybunion. In 1817 and 1818, local priest Fr Owen McCarthy went around the farming community collecting potatoes for people who were hungry and there was an acute shortage of food which spelled trouble for the area – a warning not heeded.

In the town at that time there was a fishery based on the Cashen River and fish was caught on daily basis and sold to markets in Tralee and abroad. This raises questions as to why there were so many people hungry in the area.

In 1846 it was reported that the town of Ballybunion was is a desperate state, with hundreds of people nearing starvation, and in 1847 a petition was sent to the Lord Lieutenant stating that the peaceful population was on the verge of death and desperation. The petitioners appealed to the Lord Lieutenant to increase the number on the public works schemes from 540 to four times the present total, as this would ease the suffering in the Ballybunion area. The reply from Dublin Castle stated that the legislature had otherwise provided for that object, with relief rations and soup kitchens.

The censuses of 1841 and 1851 show that the population of Killehenny, Ballybunion, was 3,050 in 1841 and that by 1851 the population had

Famine bottle, Bromore.

dropped to 1,973, either due to famine or emigration. In Killconly, north of Ballybunion, the population in 1841 was 2,210 and after the famine it had dropped to 1,521. The figures demonstrate a dramatic loss of people within the Ballybunion and Killconly townlands during and after the Great Famine, and the area never really recovered. In recent years, the number of visitors claiming to have originated from the area has increased, indicating how large the exodus was.

However, recent research has revealed that not all people in the area suffered badly during the period; in Doon and Bromore to Beal, people fished along the seashore and collected and cooked the bornachs and periwinkles and made carrigeen and sleaucan soup and people survived. It was hard in the area but people's perseverance paid off.

But for those who could not fish or were too weak, it was the workhouse in Listowel and finally Teampeall Ban graveyard, to be buried in an unmarked pauper's grave, miles from their own home town of Ballybunion. Contained within the confines of Killehenny graveyard and Killconly graveyard are the unmarked graves of famine dead. The potato crop failed in the area but fish were being exported from Ballybunion at the time, so why did so many die?

THE LOST VILLAGE OF MILLSTREET

During the Great Famine of the 1840s, thousands of people died and others were forced to leave their homes in a bid to start a new life and forget the old one. During that sad time a village just on the outskirts of Ballybunion was totally wiped from the maps of the period.

In the 1980s the author was collecting artefacts from an area called Doon Ferris and during the process a lamp was found – the area it came from was called Millstreet. This surprised everyone, but more research uncovered a hidden treasure. In an old newspaper dated from the period an account is given about the area known as Millstreet:

> Millstreet is a village at the western boundary of Ballyloughhrin, close to the Cashen estuary and Ballybunion. The inhabitants are mainly fishermen in the Cashen. Less is known perhaps of the inhabitants of this part of Ireland than any of the others. The intercourse with any large town is confined to such communication, as necessary springs from the supply they receive such articles as required for the ordinary wants of life.
>
> There's not even a good road by which the produce of the sea, their chief wealth, can be conveyed to any considerable distance. The consequence is that every article which is of native production is sold at a ruinously low price. I saw a pig hanging from one of the cottages, killed to pay the rent; it weighed eighty pounds and was offered to me for six shillings. Of course the luxuries of life, tea, sugar, clothing, are in the same ratio.

Clearly the village had either left prior to or during the Great Famine, or perhaps due to another local disaster, such as flooding. Research has shown that some people in the area had to have their beds suspended several feet off the ground at night due to flooding in the area. To this day, the picture that history paints of Millstreet remains hazy; further research is needed to uncover more about the past of this Ballybunion village.

GEORGE HEWSON, LANDLORD

The principal landlord of the Ballybunion area was George Hewson of Ennismore, Listowel. George Hewson was born in the 1800s; his mother was Mary Lysaght and his father John Hewson Esq. of Castle Hewson. George Hewson's residence was Ennismore House, Listowel. There, he and his wife Lillie and their children lived the life of the landed gentry.

In 1870, the property in the possession of the landlord was 1,208 acres in the county of Kerry. In Ballybunion, the landlord owned many properties within the town, large sections of the sandhills and fishing rites along the River Cashen, which he exploited by selling large quantities of gravel, seaweed and sand from the foreshore.

In the 1890s, George Hewson had a great interest in golf and allowed the sport to be played in the sandhills he owned in Ballyeagh, Ballybunion. Later he became one of the club's founding members and its president in 1893.

On 1 September 1882, Hewson's son Charles Lysaght Hewson was born and he was baptised at the old Killehenny Protestant church on Sandhill Road by the Rector F.G.S. Read on 27 April 1897. Elsie Hewson, the daughter of George Hewson, married Sir John McConnell, 1st Battalion, whose father was a former Lord Mayor of Belfast.

George Hewson took an interest in the welfare his tenants and was considered by many to be found in good standing; during the Black '46 in the Great Famine he gave relief to many hungry people in the Ballybunion and North Kerry.

In Ballybunion Hewson was instrumental in the development of the Castle Hotel and the Dairy, which was called Hewson's Dairy Yard. He also gave employment to many in the area on his large estate farm at Gorthnaskeha.

George Hewson's golf club.

In the late years of the 1800s, the landlord developed houses in Ballybunion, which he used as hunting and fishing lodges. Ballybunion House on Church Road was one of these and was fitted up in style each year to accommodate the guests of the landlord. This property is still in existence and is owned by Jim McMachon. In 1887, an agreement was reached with George Hewson by the Ballybunion & Listowel Railway Company to take as much sand as required from the sandhills and the foreshore at a royalty of 1*d* per ton.

George Hewson did not balk at controversy, however. He had issues with the locals on the rights of way on the Castle Green. At one stage, under the landlord's instruction, quarrying was undertaken from the cliff face of the Castle Green. Dynamite was sent for from his estate house and holes were drilled in the side of the castle; the intention was to demolish the castle and quarry the rock underneath. George Hewson was halted when locals pleaded with him and he left the remains of the castle in position. The rock under the castle was used for slabs for cold rooms of the period and for wealthy landed-gentry houses of the time. Today the drill holes for the dynamite can still be seen on the cliff face.

The landlord played his part in the tenants' rights movement by supporting a large public meeting held in Listowel in 1869, where it is said 25,000 people attended, demanding the implementation of the 'Three Fs' – Fair Rent, Freedom of Sale and Fixity of Tenure. The meeting condemned absentee landlords and those who charged high rent.

George Hewson's estate became bankrupt at the end of the 1800s and the Scottish Company took over the portfolio. The late Joseph O'Mahony of Ballybunion was the solicitor who dealt with the break-up of the estate on behalf of the company and settled many land problems which were left from the George Hewson Estate. At one stage the Scottish Company had an office in the town where residents went to pay their rent.

When George Hewson died he was buried in Dysert Graveyard, Lixnaw, not far from his beloved Ennismore House.

THE ORMSBY FAMILY

Burris Ormsby, RIC Constable

In Ballybunion, even to this day, there are many reminders of the town's military past, such as the Cashen Coastguard Station and the local Garda Station, which was formerly an RIC barracks and prior to that a hotel.

In 1834, there was another military building in the town, located on the Main Street. This building had a corrugated iron roof and a red-bricked chimney and was called the Constabulary Mess. This is where the RIC constables were based, where they had their meals and planned their daily duties in the town. Burris Ormsby was one such RIC constable and another was one William James Blundell.

The Ormsby family had a number of children born in Ballybunion: George Henry was born on 10 January 1883 and baptised on 8 February 1883 by Rector F. Read; Ann Mary Ormsby was born on 27 June 1884 and baptised on 28 June 1884 by Rector C.R. Hoggins; on 19 September 1886, another son, John James Ormsby, was born and he was baptised on 10 October 1886 by Rector Charles E. Fry; on 13 April 1889, Burris Ormsby was born and he was baptised on 1 May 1889 by Rector Charles E. Fry, and on 12 April 1890, Harriet Ellen was born and she was baptised on 11 May by Rector Charles E. Fry. All the children were baptised at the old Protestant church in Ballybunion.

Burris Ormsby and his wife Anna Maria lived for many years in the town of Ballybunion as he carried out his daily duties. Later he was transferred to Tarbert and some time after emigrated to the United States of America with his family.

During the 1990s, family members returned to Ballybunion to see where their famous ancestor was stationed. These photographs were taken of the Ormsby family in the USA. Of the photographs that remain, there are those of Burris and his wife Anna Maria and one of their daughter Harriet Ellen, who was born in Ballybunion in 1890.

Ballybunion Garda Station, formerly the RIC Barracks.

Emily Ormsby.   *Harriet Ormsby.*

THE PIPER WHO LIVED THROUGH THREE CENTURIES, 1799–1904

Tom McCarthy, the famous Ballybunion piper, was born in Doon in 1799 and tradition relates that he would wander the cliffs of Doon, listening to the wildlife around him, and on the following day he would emulate them with the pipes.

The piper's favourite place for playing was on the old Castle Green – in fact the local parish priest took on the landlord in court so that the piper and visitors had access to the castle and its vicinity. In years to follow, the piper played his uilleann pipes to all who wandered within earshot of his music and became known worldwide.

It is not known who taught Tom how to play the pipes but it is widely accepted that he started off as a war piper and graduated to the uilleann pipes. His ability to make the pipes bark like a dog and sing like the birds in his performances made him famous. One of his tunes was called 'The Hare Among the Corn'.

Throughout the life of the piper, he would be seen walking along the shoreline, as the sun was setting in the west and the waves crashed on the golden beaches of Ballybunion, thinking and planning his next day's musical arrangements. During his life, Tom McCarthy would have played for all the landed gentry in the area and at the Faction Fight at Ballyeagh. He would have played as people left the area during the Great Famine. Through the eyes of the musician, the history of Ballybunion unfolded.

On 3 August 1904, at the age of 105, Thomas McCarthy, the famous Ballybunion piper, died. He was sick for a week with a common cold, with no doctor at the time attending. Shortly after his death, his pipes were sold to an O'Sullivan man from Ballyheigue, who brought the pipes from Ballybunion. Late that night, according to legend, the pipes played of their own accord, and so O'Sullivan quickly bundled them into a bag and brought them back, saying he would not have these things in the house for any money. The pipes were brought to England

Above: *The Finuge Pipes.*

Right: *Thomas McCarthy, 1799-1904.*

51

where a family member, Martin Higgins (RIP), found the pipes and brought them back to Ireland to be restored. However, this never happened, as McCarthy's pipes vanished, and the question was raised locally: did McCarthy come back for his pipes.

THE COASTGUARD STATIONS, 1800S-1923

Located strategically on a hillside overlooking the mouth of the Cashen River were the Cashen Coastguard cottages and station. In 1824, the Irish Coastguards were established. Over 200 officers were accommodated along the coastline and some of the coastguards, like that in Beale, had temporary structures.

The Cashen Coastguard Station was well constructed with good stonework and a slated roof. All the other HM Coastguard Stations of the 1880-1923 period followed similar designs, such as those Castletownbere, Isle of Purbeck, Dorset, and Ballinskelligs.

The Cashen Coastguard Station had its own boathouse, similar in design to the boathouse of the Isle of Purbeck, Dorset, with large doors which opened outwards to facilitate quick launching. A long road led from the station on the hillside so that any approaching vessels on the estuary could be met quickly.

A large, well-constructed base for the flagstaff was constructed a short distance from the station and the flag was flown and taken down on the coastguards' daily duty. It was noted by locals that the uniform was very similar to that of the navy and this distinguished them in the area. Off duty, they wore suits which identified them when they were in Ballybunion.

In the area where the station was sited, coastguard buttons have been found from time to time, as have some of the coins and pieces of the clay pipes which the men made for themselves in a mould which bore the face of a coastguard.

Initially, in parts of Ireland (and the Cashen area was no exception), when the coastguards arrived in the area the locals were very wary of them. In their eyes they were part of the military, brought to the area to spy on them and their daily lives. However, as time went on the coastguards were accepted. In the Ballybunion area they were well known; they visited the strand and frequented the town.

Services

The Cashen Coastguard Station, in accordance with procedures, was a shoreline station, providing patrolling custom officers along the shoreline with small cutters which could enter tight inlets. Beyond the mouth of the river, the royal navy gunboats took over.

Coastguards at the Cashen Station

William Hancock Coastguard, 1882
Hugh Simson, Chief Boatman in Charge, RN, 1884
George William Oliver Boat Guard, 1885

Families at the Station

The station at the Cashen was not just a station for the military; families led their daily lives there. The coastguard cottages were comfortable and provided a safe place to bring up children. In the years 1882, 1884, 1885 and 1886, coastguards and their families at the Cashen Coastguard Station were celebrating the birth of their respective children at the station. In 1882, Samuel, son of William Hancock, was baptised and in 1884, Caroline, daughter of Hugh Simson and Francis, was born. In 1885, Rose Amelia was born to George William and Maggie Oliver. All the children were baptised at the old Killehenny church.

Cashen Coastguard Station, 1890s.

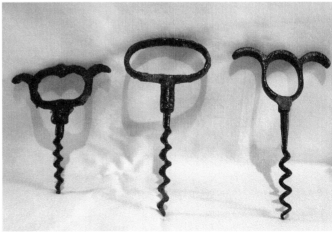

Coastguard cork screws, c. 1901.

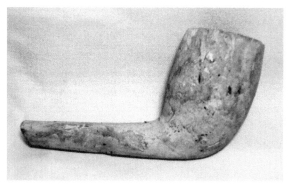

Coastguard binoculars.   *Coastguard pipe.*

In 1916 it was noticed that coastguard patrols from the Cashen Coastguard Station had increased, with the shoreline, from the mouth of the Cashen inwards, being on around-the-clock watch. According to local sources, they were on the watch for the illegal importation of arms and liquor.

The Cashen Station, like others, closed around 1923 at the dawn of the Irish Free State. The station and cottages were demolished many years ago. All that remains is the boathouse and a few artefacts such as a pair of binoculars from the 1900s, clay pipes and buttons – reminders of the days of the Cashen Coastguard Station.

Church History of Ballybunion

DOON CHURCH, 1830

North of Ballybunion, just over a mile outside the town, stands the former parish church of Ballybunion. Doon church was founded in 1830 by the Revd John Buckley, a native of Milltown, County Kerry, on a site belonging to Wilson J. Gun. The slate for the roof was brought by boat from Clare to Saleen Pier, Ballylongford, and construction was carried out by local labour. In 1833, Doon church contained one high altar of stone, the galleries, a harmonium, a sacristy, and the complete apparatus for benediction.

In 1851, Griffith's Valuation stated that the Revd James Walsh was the immediate lessor of the church. The valuation of the land and church was described as 'R.C. Chapel and yard, the A.R.P. was 0.1.6. and the land attached was valued to £18.00.'

Local sources have stated that a number of priests were brought to Doon church and buried within its sacred walls from the Penal Mass area, called Glean Na Talamh ('the Glen of the High Land'). Another story is told that when locals visited the site, the remains of only two were found and they were reinterred in Doon church. Another was buried somewhere within the

Doon church, 1930.

Doon church in ruins.

grounds of the church but there was never any marker on the grave. During the 1980s, two remains were exhumed from within the church and reinterred at the side of St John's church, Ballybunion.

In the history of Doon church we read that in February 1864, the Revd James Walsh, parish priest, died and was buried within the walls of the church. There was a plaque on the wall inside the church dedicated to Revd James Walsh but sadly this has now been removed.

The decline in Doon church was gradual; when the building of the new St John's church was completed in 1897 it was easier for much of the congregation to get to the church in the town compared with Doon church, just over a mile distant.

The gradual fall of the church came when it was closed a few times in the 1960s and '70s by Church authorities. This did not sit well with the people of the area whose ancestors built the church in poor times. Even to this day people are not happy with the way in which the former parish church was left to fall into ruin. In fact, one Sunday a small congregation came and said their prayers outside the church door, which was locked. This clearly shows the reverence in which the people from area held Doon church.

Doon church was sold to various owners over the years and at present there are plans to have the ruin converted to apartments and a small art gallery. Today all that remains is the bell, sections of a tiled floor and the cruciform-shaped structure without a roof, a sad end to a piece of our past.

THE CHURCH OF ST AUGUSTINE, RATTOO (1877-1957) & BALLYBUNION (1957-1990)

The church of St Augustine is located on Sandhill Road, Ballybunion, just a short distance from the town centre. St Augustine's was originally located in the nearby parish of Ballyduff, in an old land division called Gort Na Muin ('the Monks' Garden') located in the old barony of Clannmaurice.

St Augustine's was originally constructed 1877 by the local landlord, Wilson Gun of Rattoo. Wilson Gun was of the Gun family of Lisscahane and he had the church built as his private

St Augustine's church.

oratory for friends and workers. Prior to the construction of the church, Mass was celebrated at the Great House.

St Augustine's was a well-known landmark in Ballyduff and was well respected within the Rattoo area. It was built next to the old ecclesiastical centre of Rath Mhaighe Na Tuaiscirt, Rattoo's monastic settlement. Wilson Gun established St Augustine's during a quiet period, when the Church of Ireland was not very strong. It was stated by the Commission of Public Instruction in 1835 that the church's location was wholly inappropriate. Services were held in St Augustine's church up to the 1920s, but due to the emergence of the Irish Free State and the rapid decline of the Anglican faith, the church fell into disrepair.

New Life for St Augustine's

According to local sources, the old Killehenny church, located on a site across from the current Marine Hotel, was considered to be in a bad state of repair and it would have cost a considerable amount of money to restore. It was decided to move St Augustine's church stone by stone from Ballyduff and relocate the structure on its present site on Sandhill Road. Boyle and Harnett undertook the work; they numbered and moved each stone and rebuilt the church as it was in its original position in Rattoo – a great work of craftsmanship and building.

On 28 July 1957 (St Augustine's Day), the church was rededicated in its new environs by Revd Dr Hodges, Bishop of Limerick and Aghadoe, and the ceremony was broadcast on Raidió Éireann. By the time St Augustine's was rededicated in 1957, the Church of Ireland community in the Ballybunion area had declined, and in subsequent years its number of worshippers continued to diminish. On 1 June 1987, a ceremony was held in the church for the removal of the consecration. The building was then opened to the public on Thursday 20 December 1990 as the Ballybunion Town Library, run by the County Library Service, Kerry County Council, Tralee.

ST JOHN'S CHURCH BALLYBUNION, 1897

In the years after the arrival of the Lartigue Railway in 1888, visitors flocked in their thousands to the village of Ballybunion, so the idea of a church close to the town was deemed only proper. The former parish church at Doon was at times full, so the thorny issue of a second church was soon to become a reality.

Born near a small stream which flows into the sea near Killconly, Mary O'Malley lived with her father in a long mud house, which they shared with their chickens and one cow. Mary came of age and as there was no work in the area she went to Clare and worked in a lodging house in Killkee. It was here she met her future husband, John Young, a rich tea-plantation owner who was on holiday in the area and had just lost his wife and daughter. A romance blossomed between the couple and they got married. At this stage they lived in Dublin.

St John's church, Ballybunion.

Convent, Ballybunion.

Between 1870 and 1871, John Young died and was cremated and his ashes buried in Glasnevin Cemetery, Dublin. A story has been told locally that on the building of the O'Connell memorial, some part of John Young's grave was damaged and compensation was awarded; others say Mary claimed the place was damp. Mary O'Malley Young then exhumed the ashes of John, his first wife and daughter Margaret and moved them first to Lisslaghtin Cemetery in Ballylongford and then to Ballybunion.

It was during this time that Mary decided to stay in the area and construct the first of her two residences, which was called later Dr Hannon's. She wanted to keep young orphan girls there, but there were objections by locals. Mary then commissioned the building of the present convent and there she stayed for many years in a peaceful setting overlooking the sea.

Fr Mortimer O'Connor, the dynamic parish priest, met with Mary O'Malley at the end of the 1870s and they decided that a church would be built called St John's, named in honour of John Young. Mary O'Malley Young invested all of her fortune into the work, which commenced between the years 1891 and 1892, but early in the church's development the works were halted due to lack of finance. During these years the parish priest Fr Mortimer O'Connor was ill and taken to his bed at his residence on Cliff Road; it was not until 30 March that year that meetings were organised and there was a push to finish the church. However, Mary O'Malley Young was also very ill and she died in Dublin just before the church was finished.

In August 1897, a very frail Fr Mortimer O'Connor walked up to the altar and blessed the opening of his and Mary O'Malley Young's dream – St John's church.

Sisters of Mercy tatting, 1901.

Mary Young O'Malley's tomb.

Early Transport, Industry and Leisure in Ballybunion

BATHING BOXES OF THE 1890S

In the 1890s there were many developments in the town, as the new railway increased visitor numbers from just a few hundred in the early part of the 1800s to daily excursions numbering in the thousands. Ballybunion was now establishing itself as a visitor town.

Along the seafront at the time there were no toilets or shelters for bathers. A solution was found in the introduction of bathing boxes. In Victorian times, the use of portable bathing machines or bathing boxes was common. The four-wheeled machine was pulled by a horse or donkey to the water's edge and there, in total privacy, the bather was helped into the water to enjoy the healthy experience. In the interests of privacy, the bathing boxes were lined along the strand in ranks, and in 1890 there were eight bathing boxes in rank operating on the strand in Ballybunion.

Bathing Boxes, 1890s.

The door of the bathing box faced the sea at all times to allow privacy for the men and safeguard the dignity of the female bathers, which at that time was paramount in the eyes of the local priests and the founding fathers of the town. A small window allowed some light into the bathing box, towels were hung from the rails on the exterior of the box, a modest fee was charged and everyone was extremely happy.

Due to the design of the bathing box, the four-wheeled machine was easy to move; the mowing machine wheels were wide to enough cross the dry or wet sand on the beach and in the evening the boxes were parked on the bend of the road leading to the ladies' strand.

The bathing boxes were operated by families who became as famous as the town itself. At the end of the 1800s it was operated by Danahers and in the 1960s other locals operated the bathing boxes, most famously Brig Downey of Ahafona.

In 1951, there were more than fourteen bathing boxes on the strand, which saw the operation at its height. But as times progressed and values changed, the bathing boxes were no longer needed and they became unprofitable. The boxes finally left the beaches in the 1960s and '70s, never to return. Most of them were broken up and scrapped; only a few wall sections are still visible in the area, used for shuttering.

SHIPS AND RIVERBOATS OF THE SHANNON

Ghost Ships that Sailed the Shannon

At 9 p.m. on Saturday night, 26 November 1898, the 537 ton SS *Premier*, under Captain Murray and seventeen crew, headed into the estuary towards Beale, laden with a cargo of sugar from the port of Hamburg *en route* to the port of Limerick.

Captain Murray decided to anchor just off the Island of Scattery that night and wait until the morning tide to proceed upriver to the port of Limerick. On the morning of 27 November, the anchor was drawn and the SS *Premier* moved slowly on up the river. The vessel was proceeding under steam as the sails were not used due to the prevailing north-east wind. On board the crew were happy that a long shore break awaited them. However, this was not to be the outcome.

The *Mermaid* was, at this time, making its outward voyage from the port of Limerick and was relieving the paddle steamer the *Shannon*, which at the time was being repaired at port.

The weather was clear as Captain Murray steered the *Premier* up the estuary, in fact it was stated that the weather was 'tolerable fair sea running' at the time. It is not clear what happened next, but the reports state that Captain Murray spotted the *Mermaid* coming in his direction and he sounded the alarm, with a whistle alerting the crew to take evasive action, but it was too late; the 150 ton *Mermaid* collided with the *Premier* port side, penetrating up to 12ft into the ship, causing the waters of the estuary to flow in, crippling the steamer.

Two lifeboats were lowered from the *Premier* and the crew abandoned ship in the estuary. Within minutes the SS *Premier* sank beneath the waves of the Shannon to a depth of seventeen fathoms. The *Mermaid* crew also abandoned ship, but according to the report they returned and brought her slowly back to port.

A vessel on the Shannon at sunset.

The crew of the *Premier* were later brought on board the SS *Vanda*, under command of Captain Walton, which was *en route* to Limerick with a cargo of flour for a Messrs McGuire. In port, the crew were taken care of by the local Mariners' Society.

At the time, no inquiry was held. According to reports of the period, no pilots were used. There were depositions made by both crews at the court house on the Monday following the collision. The underwriters paid in full for the loss of the SS *Premier*; no salvage was carried out on the wreck due to the depth of seventeen fathoms and the nature of the cargo of sugar. When the *Premier* sank, it lay under 6oft of water in an area which was not at the time going to cause a hazard to navigation of the shipping lane. The SS *Premier* was not entered into the harbour records and was not subjected to pilot or harbour dues. Thus, the sugar boat SS *Premier* faded into memory and the pages of history.

In 1978, a wreck was uncovered by sonic investigations and later by a diver called John Power. Power found a brass ship's bell engraved with the word 'Premier' and a plate with the name of the ship's agents, Lloyds of London, who were contacted. It was indeed the *Premier*. One of the ghost ships of the Shannon had been found.

The SS Premier *Facts*
The steamship was built in 1894 by a Scottish shipbuilder called John Shearer & Son, Glasgow. The *Premier* was owned by Messrs J. Simson. She was 537 tons gross and 175ft long, with a 25ft beam and a 10ft 10in draft. She was rigged and she was a three-masted schooner.

The Mermaid *Facts*

The 153-ton-gross *Mermaid* was built in 1864 in Glasgow by Messrs Twingate & Co. and was owned by the Waterford Steam Ship Company. The ship was 161ft long, had a 19ft beam and she drew 8ft under the command of Captain Cotter of Waterford.

The Riverboats of the Shannon, 1921

In the early 1900s, the Shannon estuary was used to its maximum to transport goods from Kilrush to Foynes and down the coast to Saleen Pier at Ballylongford. Long before the increase in road transport and the arrival of large trucks, riverboats from Kilrush sailed the Shannon and across the estuary daily with their cargos.

In the Ballybunion area, many old items of the past which were brought from County Clare remain and are a reminder of how the riverboats contributed to the area. Clothing, furniture and fertiliser were all brought into the Ballybunion area from Clare via Saleen Pier.

Saleen Pier

Saleen Pier, near Ballylongford, was the place to which the goods were brought from Clare. This commenced around 1921 with the establishment of the Shannon Express Company, which was founded by David Sullivan from Ballylongford and the late Dan Ryan from Kilrush. Two other founders and directors of the company were from Tarbert and Glin.

Pulley winch on Saleen Pier.

Scattery Island.

Oil lamps from the 1930s.

The EDJ

The cargo boat *EDJ* (*c.*1921) was constructed of steel, had a hot bulb engine, and came from the south of England. The *EDJ* could carry up to 100 tons when laden. It was during the Civil War period that the boat operated along the Shannon and the trouble of this period had an effect on the Shannon. The company went out of business and later the *EDJ* was sold to Glynns, Kilrush, and then she was sold on to O'Keeffe of Bantry. The boat eventually made its way back to the Shannon under local ownership in Ballylongford. The *EDJ*, while carrying a load of turf to Limerick during the war period, ran onto the rocks near Cappa Pier. The boat was later moved to Tarbert and subsequently broken up.

The Shannon Steam Co. Ltd of Killrush was owned by the Glynn family and traded on the river from the 1920s onwards. This family gave employment to many in the area and contributed a great deal to the economy of Kilrush and North Kerry in those bygone days.

The company carried all types of cargo; the bulk was wheat and maize from Limerick to the family flour and feed mills based at Kilrush. The grain was milled there and the final products, flour, bran, pollard, meal and other animal feeds, were loaded on to their boats and distributed to stores along the river at Tarbert Island, Glin and Mount Kenneth Quay, Limerick. The family also had a store at Saleen Pier at Ballylongford.

The Corona

The *Corona* was a steamer and could carry up to 120 tons. This boat carried out a steady trade on the river and belonged to the Shannon Steamship Company of Kilrush, owned by the Glynn family. The boat was broken up near Cappa Pier before the Second World War.

The Indium

Owned by the Imperial Chemical Industries, this small sturdy steamer was purchased by the Glynns after the *Corona* and carried tons of Irish wheat to Limerick and Kilrush during the war years.

The Dingle

The *Dingle* was owned by the Limerick Steamship Company and carried goods from the coastal steamer at Fenit up the shallow canal to Tralee. She was used to transport turf from Killrush to Limerick during the war. Later, the *Dingle* was sold to Glynns, where she transported wheat and barley from Limerick to the estuary. The *Dingle* was a barge type and it has been said that barges like the *Dingle* were used by the troops at Gallipoli.

The St Senan, *formerly the* Enterprise.

This boat could carry 50 tons and was 50ft long. It was built by Tyrrels of Arklow in 1921 for John Walsh of Foynes. The boat had a hot bulb Widdop oil engine originally, but later a Kelvin diesel engine was fitted. When the boat was launched it was called the *Enterprise* but this was later changed to the *St Senan*. The vessel was sold to St Senan Carriers Ltd of Kilrush and later scrapped at Kilrush.

The Indus

The boat associated with Saleen was called the *Indus* and was owned by Mr David Walsh of Labasheeda. This vessel traded between the port of Limerick Foynes and Saleen Pier and Kildysert. Coaster cargos of 300 to 400 tons of fertiliser was brought to Saleen Pier and distributed to the farms in North Kerry.

The company closed its last store in Limerick in the 1960s. Saleen had closed earlier, as river transport lost out to road transport. The tide had turned for the riverboats that sailed the Shannon.

Shipwrecks of the Ballybunion Area 1800s

The rugged coastline of Ballybunion to Beal was, at one time during the 1800s, strewn with the wreckage of sailing ships and steamers which went aground or were lured onto the rocks. While the history surrounding some of the shipwrecks in the area is vague, many accounts and stories exist, as do artefacts from the period.

The City of Limerick

The *City of Limerick* was wrecked on the Long Strand on 28 December 1833. The ship was *en route* to London from the port of Limerick.

Wreck area of the City of Limerick.

The Sea Lark

On 25 November 1846, the *Sea Lark*, which was Limerick owned, was brought onto the rocks by stormy weather. In the history of the area, the *Sea Lark* is well known. Tradition relates that on the night that the *Lark* hit the reef of rocks just below the Blackrocks, most of crew of the ship drowned and they were buried within the sand dunes where the Cashen Golf Course is now.

The *Sea Lark*'s captain and a cabin boy supposedly survived the wreck and were put up in houses in the Ballybunion area. It was said that when the captain went down the following day to view the remains of the *Sea Lark* he stated, 'Oh Lark! Oh Lark! Your nest has been robbed!' Overnight, locals in the area pillaged the wreck and left the *Sea Lark* in a ruined state. The marks where the *Sea Lark* went ashore along the reef can still be seen to this day.

The Senator

I heard the old people talk about the *Senator*; it was wrecked along the same area as the two previously mentioned ships.

The Ileen

The schooner the *Ileen* was wrecked within this same area, but some locals have informed me that it was wrecked near the Cashen mouth on 6 October 1889.

Llanthenry, *1902*

In the Beal area, one ship has been etched into the memory: the *Llanthenry*, a steamer which went aground on Beal Bar on 27 December 1902. All ten crew survived but the ship was a total wreck, according to the Lloyd representative at the time. The 148 ton vessel was *en route* from Garston to Limerick with coal. All that remains of the ship are pieces of copper pipe which the author has preserved.

The Thetis, *1834*

During the winter months each year, the remains of the *Thetis* can be seen at low tide, in the spot where she went aground on Beale Bar on 30 November 1834. The ship is also marked on the Ordnance Survey maps of the area. The *Thetis* was, like the other ships, *en route* to the port of Limerick.

The Dronningen *or* Celestial Queen, *1864-1882*

In the Ballybunion area, one wreck stands out: the 837 ton barque the *Dronningen*. She was built in Sunderland in 1864 and owned by J.L. Johanson & Co., Christiania (Oslo), Norway. In 1878, the ship was known as the *Celestial Queen* and was owned by Pile & Co., London (1864-1878) and Park Brothers of London (1878). The ship was originally fitted out as a fully rigged vessel and in 1879 the *Dronningen* was rebuilt as a barque.

The *Dronningen* left Glasgow for New York on 11 November 1882, fully laden with a cargo of 1,000 tons of Gas Kennel Coal to be used for the powering of the generators of the city. The ship and its crew found themselves caught in the eye of a hurricane just off the coast of Ireland and according to historians of the area the crew were drifting for days without food until they spotted land. The ship was pushed towards the Clare side, and then, with the massive waves, was brought onto the rocks just south of Lick Castle in an area call Bun Na Trogha, late on the night of 20 November 1882.

Locals brought ropes out to the cliff edge to aid the stricken ship and crew. All were brought ashore safely, where they stayed the night in local houses and were treated well by the people

of the area. The following day the crew went back to the wreck and tried to claim back some of their personal items, but some were lost to the sea forever.

Coal from the
Dronningen.

Wreck Auction, 4 December 1882

On Monday 4 December 1882, an auction was held in Ballybunion for the purpose of selling the remains of the 837 ton barque. Among the items were ropes, sails, copper sheeting, rigging, chains, tow ropes and tons of Gas Kennel Coal, and they were sold in lots to the highest bidder. McElligott and Shine were the auctioneers and Robert McCowen Esq., Tralee, was the Lloyd's Agent.

In the decades that followed, items such as tables, coal and anchors were discovered in the area, and indeed many a horseshoe was made in Jack Leahy's forge in Bromore from the large chains once used by the crew of the *Dronningen*.

THE CASTLE HOTEL

It is said that the Castle Hotel was originally used as a hunting lodge and fishing lodge by the town's landlord George Hewson, who had fishing rights along the Cashen estuary. A newspaper advertisement dated 20 May 1874 stated that the Castle Hotel Ballybunion was 'now open'. In the century that followed, the hotel would play a vital role in the development of the town, its golf course and the Lartigue Monorail.

The hotel was constructed on an elevated site with exceptional views of the ladies' beach and scenic cliffs. The residents had their own access to the foreshore, which at that time was considered the unique benefit to staying at the Castle Hotel. A small putting green was constructed at the front of the hotel and it had its own tennis court, which was grassed. Both of these features were well used during the life of the castle.

The reputation of the hotel grew steadily, as more and more landed gentry visited the town to take to the waters and enjoy the champagne air of Ballybunion. In the locality, this meant employment, and over the lifetime of the Castle Hotel, many locals worked there as maids, cooks, doormen, and maintenance staff. The hotel was regarded as the elite place to stay and no local would venture in or even look over the wall; this was the Hilton of yesteryear. However, the hotel did purchase its milk, butter and all its daily stock from the Ballybunion area, so the farming community and business people did benefit from its development.

In the later stages of the 1800s, the plans for the new railway – the Lartigue Monorail – were in full motion, which meant that the

Castle Hotel, Ballybunion.

Castle Hotel, 1927.

Castle Hotel, 1990s.

Castle Hotel would have the benefit of a rail link to the market town of Listowel, enabling more visitors to stay in Ballybunion. In 1888, the rail line opened and the numbers of visitors to the new hotel increased. Indeed, the Castle Hotel was well positioned at the turn of the century.

On 18 August 1893, the opening meeting of Ballybunion Golf Club took place at the hotel. At this stage, twelve greens were constructed on the golf course and the hotel was in prime position to take the golfing enthusiasts who would arrive on the Lartigue from the Listowel Station. Indeed, no sooner than the reputation of the links became known, golfers were staying there and at the other hotels in the town. The Castle was now in full operation and Ballybunion was reaping the benefits of a first-class hotel and golf course.

During the summer months, the Castle Hotel became popular with visitors who liked to venture into the caves and onto the cliff walks (which were many). The annual Pattern Day, 15 August, became a great occasion and the hotel catered for those who came to the resort at the time.

The Castle Hotel prospered down through the decades, until the emergence of the Irish Free State in 1924, which saw the hotel come under gunfire from republican forces due to the fact that it was used to store ammunition and as a base for Free State troops. The chimneys of the Castle were bullet-holed from this conflict and at one stage the hotel was burned on its southern front so badly that sections of roof had to be replaced.

In 1924, the Castle Hotel saw the end of its connection with the Lartigue Railway when the line closed due to the damage sustained during the Civil War and subsequent heavy losses. The Castle Hotel and other hotels in Ballybunion faced an uncertain future, but due to modern modes of transport and the reputation of the hotel, people returned and stayed at the Castle Hotel and in Ballybunion again. In the thirty-year period from the 1940s, the Castle Hotel prospered and so did the town.

Until the 1990s, the Castle Hotel continued to be held in high regard by all those visitors who stayed there. In fact, many visitors returned each year to stay and enjoy the old Castle. At the end of the 1990s, plans were drawn up to build a new, state-of-the-art hotel on the site, and it was at this stage that the old Castle Hotel was knocked down and quietly slipped into the pages of Ballybunion's history, only to seen in old photographs and postcards. In recent times, artefacts such as a key from the door of the Castle Hotel and old menus have been found, serving as reminders of Ballybunion's hotel history.

Castle Hotel Ballybunion, 1900s.

THE LARTIGUE MONORAIL SYSTEM, 1888–1924

The Origins of the Lartigue Monorail

Charles Francois Marie Theresa Lartigue, a French railway pioneer, based his early monorail ideas on the movement of camels on rough terrain. Their bodies were the driving force and the way they moved gave the designer the idea of the A-shaped track with a load slug either side in a pannier fashion. The birth of the Lartigue monorail system had begun.

In 1888, a demonstration line was set up in London near Victoria Street in a site now occupied by Westminster Cathedral. On display were lines and turntables designed by Lartigue and Anatole Mallet, the great locomotive designer who also would put his hallmark on the project. In 1894, a Lartigue line operated from Feurs to Panissiere in Central France. Lartigue lines were also operating at the Ria mines near St Petersburg in Russia, in Peru and in Guatemala.

The local parish priest, Fr Mortimer O'Connor, canvased all known local bodies at the time to put in place a railway to link the town of Ballybunion to the market town of Listowel. His initiative was the corner stone for the development of the Lartigue Railway.

Parliamentary Bill, 1886

All the lobbying was successful. On 2 April 1886, a Parliamentary Bill before the House of Commons in London passed its second reading. The Royal Accent was granted on 16 April 1886 and the Ballybunion & Listowel Railway Company was incorporated on that day.

The sum allocated by the Bill of Parliament was £33,000. The Chairman was the Right Honourable Earl of Devon and on 16 June 1887 a prospectus on the line was published. The dream was becoming a reality, and in the autumn of 1887, work commenced on the 'Permanent Way'. Ballybunion's monorail system would go down in history as the first commercial monorail in the British Isles.

The Lartigue line ran for nine miles from Listowel to Ballybunion and stopped halfway at Lisselton Station. The land was acquired along the route from local farmers who co-operated

Lartigue Monorail, 1888.

with the railway. The railway company finished the work well within the allocated budget. The original locomotive that featured in the early demonstration was used to build the new line. This locomotive was called the *Coffee Pot*; it weighed 2½ tons and had a speed of six miles per hour. The *Coffee Pot* was left in a shed in Listowel for many years and was sold to an individual from Tarbert around the 1900s.

In 1887, the Hunslet locomotive builders received orders from the Listowel & Ballybunion Company to build three 0-3-0 tender engines which would drive the famous Lartigue system. Goods and passenger coaches were constructed by Messrs Achilles Legrand of Mons, Belgium, twenty-one in all.

Overbridges

Overbridges were constructed at Ahafona and on the Gortaskeha road, but only one is still in existence today. A timber footbridge at the rear of O'Connor's bar (Kilcooley's) was constructed to facilitate passengers.

Above: *Overbridge, Gornaskeha.*

Left: *Lartigue flying gate wheel, 1888.*

Turntables

Turntables were used in the Ballybunion area due to the nature of the design. Located at Ahafona and adjacent to the station house in Ballybunion, these moving tables were employed for shunting wagons and were used as additional spurs at both station houses. Turntables were manually operated by two or three people. At both ends of the table, mechanisms kept the tables locked. When they were unlocked, the table moved on wheels, so a locomotive or any of the Lartigue rolling stock could be rotated quickly at any time. During the 1980s, the site on which Kit Ahern (RIP) lived was excavated and a full section of a turntable was unearthed.

The Station House

The station house in Ballybunion was constructed in 1888 from corrugated iron, as were the ancillary buildings. The station house was later blown up by republican forces during the Civil War. The station was equipped with turntables, sidings, workshops and a spur to collect sand from the golf course.

In 1888, the Lartigue Monorail line was completed. The official date of the opening was set by the company for 29 February that year. Due to modifications to the braking system ordered by General Hutchinson, the first train (which only carried ballast) from Ballybunion to Listowel travelled on 28 February 1888.

The Official Opening, 29 February 1888

The day had arrived and dignitaries from all over the British Isles were in attendance when, shortly after twelve noon, the Lartigue Monorail departed the Listowel Station on its official journey to Ballybunion.

The journey took thirty-five minutes and some passengers complained about the noise from the wheels located just behind them. Behr told them that this noise would disappear over time but of course it did not as it was a characteristic of the rolling stock.

It was a dream come true for Lartigue and Anatole Mallet; their work was there for all to see and to be respected by railway companies worldwide. Ballybunion Station was adorned with bunting that day and as it waited for the locomotive to arrive and a friendly carnival atmosphere was prevalent. This was Ballybunion's finest hour; the town could now market itself well and a encourage visitors to come to the seaside resort of the west. The official party was treated to a walk along the cliffs and the history of the area was told. They were extended the hospitality of the town and a reception was held in the station house, where speeches were heard from the visiting dignitaries.

The Lartigue Monorail then left the station in Ballybunion *en route* to Listowel, but had to stop due to the overheating of an axle. The official party retired for the evening to Killarney, where the dignitaries heard Charles Lartigue speak in his native French about how impressed he had been with the work carried out by the railway company on the construction of his monorail system.

The Lartigue came into public use on 5 March 1888, driven by Mr Joseph Hollyoake. The Hollyoake family would be connected with the Lartigue Monorail over the duration of its life.

A history of the Lartigue Monorail would not be complete without mention of one of its favourite sons and a person who would leave a dynamic mark on the railway's history. Mr Patrick McCarthy was born in Lixnaw, County Kerry, in 1862. He received his education on the Limerick and Waterford and Western Railways. In 1888 he became station master at Listowel and accountant to the railway company, and in October 1890 he was elevated to the role of General Manager. He was determined to make the Lartigue profitable and, with his hard work, Ballybunion emerged as a unique seaside town in North Kerry.

The A-Shaped Track

The construction of the noted A-shaped track formation was unique; it has been stated that Lartigue got the idea from camels crossing the desert, as their feet never got stuck in the sand. Similarly, the pannier style in which goods were transported was said to be based on the camels.

The line took several months to construct – the running rail was 27lb per yard in 3ft lengths and this was secured to the A-shaped track angle iron at the base by iron sleepers which were bolted to a wooden sleeper. At various sections, the St Andrew's Cross was inserted to avoid creeping and to stop track movement. Additional rails called guide rails were used. These were 11lb per yard in 20ft lengths and were bolted and later clamped to the ends of the angle iron. Their purpose was to give rolling stock and locomotive balance. Double-flanged wheels were used in all of the rolling stock.

In the end, this light but strong construction was suitable for the line from Listowel to Ballybunion and proved that the monorail could adapt to any change in ground level, such as rivers, steep banks and ravines.

Locomotives and Passenger Wagons

Three locomotives were constructed by Hunslet of Leeds. In October 1887, a track was constructed by the company to test the newly built locomotives. Each of the three locomotives had a Lartigue and Mallet logo on the side and according to Lartigue historians the colours were green and red. After these company tests, the locomotives were dismantled and shipped to Listowel to be reassembled. The *Coffee Pot* locomotive which was used in the construction of the line was sold and dismantled in Tarbert when the railway was in full operation in 1888.

Rolling Stock

The first, second, third and sand wagons were constructed by the well-known Messrs Achille Legrand firm of Mons, Belgium. The roofs tilted inward and all the coaches were pannier-style, so step bridges were used to gain access to both sides of the locomotive. A piece of material was used to cover the windows in order to kill the glare of the sunlight.

The Lartigue coaches were bolted to a box-shaped construction containing flanged wheels on the top and guide wheels along the base. A coach builder called Maurice Nugent was employed to fix any damaged rolling stock.

Sand Wagons or Sand hoppers

Twenty sand hoppers were used to transport thousand of tons of sand from the pit located on the golf course, just below what was called the railway gap. Permission was obtained from the local landlord George Hewson. Each wagon carried two half tons with 200 tons being transported to Listowel daily.

Flying Gates

Seventeen very unusual drawbridges were built between Listowel and Ballybunion; their purpose was to allow farmers whose land bordered the crossings to pass over the track unhindered. When the flying gates were activated, a signal arm was raised, thus warning the oncoming train that the gate was in use.

These gates were located at Ahafona and at McDonald's, Gorthnaskeha, but all that remains of these gates is one of the flying-gate wheels, which is now in the possession of the author.

The Demise of the Lartigue Monorail

In 1921, the Ballybunion area was in a state of unrest. The monorail was in a poor state] and was a prime target for anti-government action, according to *The Kerry People* of July 1921. In September of that year, a masked gunman held up the Lartigue and stole mailbags *en route* to Ballybunion. The English military ordered the temporary closure of the Lartigue, but after a short period the line reopened.

In 1920, the British government relinquished all claims on the railways in Ireland, resulting in rising costs in wages and replacing locomotives and rolling stock, all of which had its effect on the Lartigue. During the Civil War the Lartigue was badly damaged because the Free State Troops used the railway on a daily basis. Ballybunion Station was blown up and occupational crossings were opened, allowing the Lartigue Locomotive No.1 to be derailed near where John O'Connor's Hotel stands today. Other aggressions included the unbolting of tracks, which again added to costs, and the rolling stock was damaged. Sadly, due to the fact that it received no state support, the climate in the country at the time, the losses it was taking, and the poor service offered to customers due breakdowns during busy days, the Lartigue was nearing the end of its life.

At a 1924 meeting in Ballybunion, the Improvements Committee tried in vain to lobby the government to save the line and the jobs, and they stressed potential losses to the area, but it all fell on deaf ears. An application was made on 7 October 1924 by the general manager and receiver to wind up the company, after all efforts had proved unsuccessful. The order was granted and on the fourteenth day of that month, Mr Michael Hollyoake drove the Lartigue into the engine shed in Listowel. Thomas Ward of Sheffield scrapped the line from Ballybunion to Lisselton and finally to Listowel. All locomotives were reduced to scrap and sold in lots; the majority was shipped to England to be melted down. The Lartigue Monorail was now gone forever, and with it, Charles Lartigue's dream.

In modern times, great credit is due to my friend and local historian Michael Barry, who restored a section of the track. It was an immense achievement which deserves our thanks. The author has a section which is under construction, along with some artefacts relating to the Lartigue. In Listowel today, the Lartigue Committee has rebuilt a diesel engine replica running adjacent to the original track, which is well worth the visit.

BALLYBUNION GOLF CLUB

The inaugural meeting of Ballybunion Golf Club took place at the Castle Hotel on 18 August 1893. Among those in attendance at that historic meeting were Mr Creagh, Listowel, and Mr Carling, who were nominated as Vice-Presidents, and it was agreed to ask Lord Listowel to allow his name go forward as President. The prestigious position of Honorary Secretary was given to Mr Darcy of Ballybunion.

During the inaugural meeting of the newly established committee, the club proposed a vote of thanks to George Hewson, JP, Ennismore, who permitted the use of his land for golf rent free. This fact excited the meeting; golfers could travel by rail, stay at the first-class Castle Hotel, and walk the short distance to the first tee.

Ballybunion Golf Club, old first green.

Twelve greens had been constructed upon Hewson's land, but over time the links were upgraded to the full eighteen. Additional greens, bunkers and fairways were to be added if the members so wished, thus developing a golfing paradise.

This early course was described in 1893, 'the greens all lie among the sandhills, the turf is of the springiest, and the course offers every variety of golfing interest'. In that respect, visiting golfers were requested to book their tee times at the newly established Ballybunion Golf Club by contacting the treasurer, Mr N. Darcy in Ballybunion.

In 1893, George Hewson was offered the position of Acting President and it was at this time that he let the ground to the club for the fee of £10 per year, with the first three years at £1. It was also agreed that George Hewson and his family would have full membership without paying a yearly subscription.

The Development of a Gem

The development of the early course was left to a few hands but these hands polished a diamond which would last forever. The Lartigue Railway Company, in encouraging passengers to travel to Ballybunion and in bringing a professional down to lay out the primitive course in 1892, was pivotal in creating the full course.

Many pioneering architects have been mentioned in the development of the club, such as Captain Lionel Hewson, who, according to local sources, was invited by Colonel Bartholomew to advise on the course. Historical facts point to one company, Simson & Gourlay, who surveyed the course and took into consideration what had been laid down before them. In fact, they added their unique touch to the old eighteen-hole course. Great credit is due to all who worked on the original course and those who do to this day.

Captains

The first captain of Ballybunion Golf Club was the Very Revd Canon R.A. Adderly. Mrs Rosalie Venn (*née* Shortis) was the first Lady Captain in 1941 and her daughter Angela Gilmore became Lady Captain in 1971, continuing the family's connection with the club.

One family had a unique association with the club – the Allen family. Tom Allen was employed by the club as a caretaker in 1911 on a weekly wage of 3*s*. His daily duties included golf club rentals and the sale of balls to visiting golfers. Tom's horse Nancy was well known in the area for predicting the weather; when not pulling the mowers to cut the fairways, Nancy would come closer to the club house if rain was imminent.

Ballybunion Golf Club has had an illustrious list of professionals, even since its humble beginnings. The first was Maurice Moses O'Neill, a former Irish Champion in 1923, '24 and '25. He was employed by the club in 1932 and 1933. Maurice was regarded as a great teacher of the game and was instrumental in the redesign of various holes on the course. Daniel Murray, Denis Cassidy (1936-37), Gerry Brown, John Doran (1939-40), Collins, O'Sullivan, Higgins and Finnegan were professionals up to 1967, when local man Brendan Houlihan took over.

Brendan Houlihan was, like Maurice Moses O'Neill, regarded as being a great teacher of the game of golf and he was well respected and liked. Brendan was the professional until 1978, when Ted Higgins assumed the position.

In modern times, the club has hosted various visiting world-famous golfers. Masters Champion Tom Watson is highly regarded in Ballybunion and visited the club during the 1970s and '80s on numerous occasions prior to his games at the British Open. Other golfing giants who walked the greens of Ballybunion include Byron Nelson, Tip O'Neill, Jack Nicklaus, Peter Thomson and Christy O'Connor Snr.

During the war years of the 1940s, all golf clubs, including Ballybunion, were rationed golf balls marked 'remould' or 'RM', which were circulated to the clubs by the Dunlop rubber company.

Ballybunion in the 1900s

SEAWEED BATHS OF BALLYBUNION

At the turn of the nineteenth century, seaweed baths were opened along the seafront on the ladies' strand. Seaweed was procured from the rocks along the seashore and used for its curative and health properties, and in time Ballybunion became renowned worldwide for its promotion of health through its seaweed-bath culture.

This unique attraction brought more visitors to Ballybunion, where daily lives centred on the farm or in city industries; a long soak in one of the two baths followed by a swim in the sea rejuvenated their skin and helped in the prevention of arthritis and other aging problems.

The seaweed was obtained from the rocks at the Black Rocks (or Lac Boy as it was then called) and carried by donkey and cart to heaps near the baths, ready to be used. This natural material was clearly and asset to the town, as alongside its health properties, it was also used for fertiliser on farms and other applications.

Ladies' Strand, 1900s.

Right: *Daly's seaweed baths.*

Below left: *A boiler from one of Daly's seaweed baths.*

Below right: *Collins's seaweed baths.*

In the town of Ballybunion and abroad, two families were to become synonymous with the promotion of the seaweed-bath culture: the Dalys and the Collins. These two families took great care of their patrons and contributed to the development of the beach and seafront for years. Tourists would visit these baths and leave the area happy, and so they would return to Ballybunion on an annual basis. Many famous individuals visited the baths, and because they could do so without being spotted or hassled, they would tell their friends about the Ballybunion baths and so they gave the area valuable publicity.

Today, the seaweed baths are still in operation. They are run by the Mulvihills, ancestors of the Collins family, and visitors still receive the same high level of service that was delivered 100 years ago. Daly's baths closed a few years ago and are due to be knocked down in the near future to make way for apartments, thus closing the chapter in one family's great history.

Kerry Football Team, 1929. (Image courtesy of Heritage Archive)

BOB STACK, ALL-IRELAND FOOTBALL CHAMPION

Born in New York in 1901, Bob Stack was a son of J.R. Stack and his wife Mary. The family had emigrated from Ireland in the 1880s but they returned to their home in Doon many years later. In County Kerry, Bob Stack was highly regarded as a footballer; his well-built physique and football skills made him a giant on any team, local or county. Many titles were won by Bob Stack's teams. All-Ireland medals, Railway Cups, National League titles and a collection of North Kerry titles made him famous for football.

North Kerry's six-time All-Ireland Football Champion Bob Stack died on 20 September 1976 and left behind him a legacy of football memories for the future generations of North Kerry footballers. On Sunday 9 July 1989, Pairc De Staic was officially opened by GAA officials and dedicated to the memory of Bob Stack.

BALLYBUNION COURTHOUSE MEETING, 1908

On 13 October 1908, at a packed court house on Main Street, Ballybunion, a subcommittee was formed to highlight the plight of pensioners in the area. This committee was spearheaded by well-known people in the Ballybunion area and proved successful.

In the minute book, the opening meeting transcript reads:

The first meeting of the Lisselton Sub Committee on Old Age Pensions was held at the Courthouse Ballybunion on the aforesaid date.

The chief business of the meeting was the election of a Chairman, Clerk and to fix the place for the meeting in future. For Chairman Very Revd Canon Molyneaux proposed by Revd Canon Hayes seconded by Garrett Pierce elected unanimously.

The Chairman thanked the members for his unanimous election; he was sure his work would be made light and easy by the intelligent committee which he would have working with him, and he was certain they would all co-operate to extract from the British Treasury every penny possible legally for the benefit of the old people.

There were two proposals for Clerk: John Pierce and Daniel Boland. John Pierce was proposed by Canon Hayes and was seconded by Timothy Sullivan. John Pierce was declared elected.

A resolution was then proposed by the late Garrett Pierce, that we, the members of the Lisselton Sub Committee County of Kerry on Old Age Pensions, at this our first meeting do strongly protest against the action of the government in excluding these poor people who are

Ballybunion Oct. 13th 1908
The first meeting of Liselton Sub-Committee
on Old Age Pensions was held at the
Courthouse Ballybunion on above date
The chief business of the meeting
was the election of Chairman Clerk
and to fix the place of meeting in future.
For Chairman Very Rev. Canon Molyneaux
proposed by Very Rev. Canon Hayes seconded
by Garrett Pierse M.C.C. elected unanimously
The Chairman thanked the members
for his unanimous election and he was
sure that his work would be made
light and easy by the intelligent committee which he would have working
with him and he was certain they
would all cooperate to extract from
the British Treasury every penny possible
legally for the benefit of the old people
There were two applicants for Clerk
viz John Pierse and Daniel Boland
Very Rev. Canon Hayes proposed
John Pierse for Clerk and Timothy
Sullivan D.C. seconded and Mr
Boland being not proposed, John

Court House book, 1908.

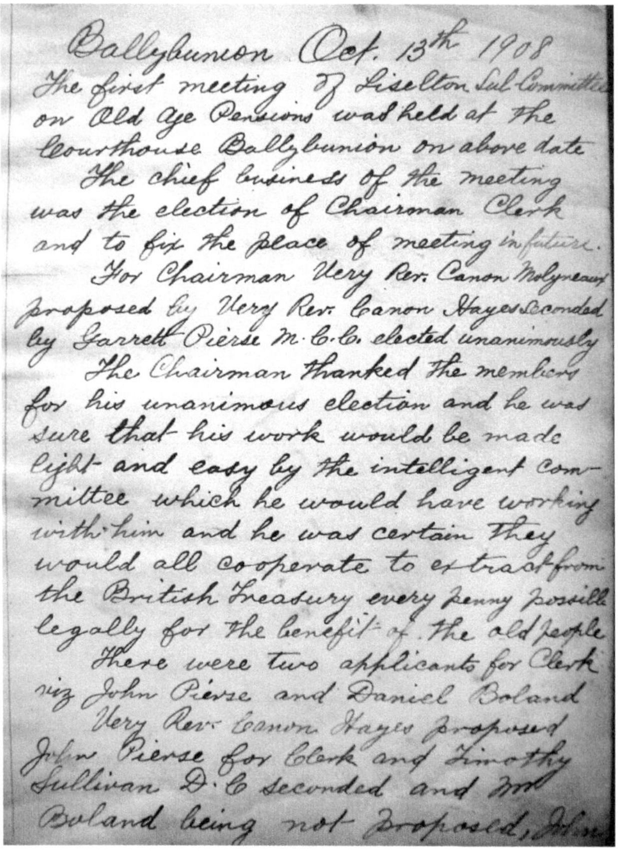

Pension book, 1908.

in receipt of Outdoor Relief of the Old Age Pensions Act and who have fulfilled the statutory conditions otherwise, and that we earnestly hope that the government will at an early date amend the Act so as to include this most deserving class of the community and that copies of this resolution be sent to the press, John E. Redmond, M. Flavin and Augustine Birrell, Chief Secretary for Ireland.

Signed,
John Canon Molyneaux, PP.

BALLYBUNION IMPROVEMENTS, 1912

In 1912, concerns of the business people over the state of the town came to a head. Prominent business interests held a meeting in the town to form a committee to raise the necessary funds to enhance and to develop the town in line with other resorts. The committee elected included the Very Revd Canon Fuller, PP; William O'Carroll, honorary secretary; and treasurers Joseph Costello, MD; P. McCarthy; Revd G.A. Hewson, MA, Rector; Revd J. Dillion, CC; Revd O'Shea, CC; P. O'Carroll, JP, and D.M. Rattary, JP.

In an open letter posted to advertising boards at the time, the Honorary Secretary William O'Carroll outlined the committee's wish to develop the town of Ballybunion:

Ballybunion, Co. Kerry
March 1917

Dear Sir or Madame,

A Committee has been formed for carrying out a number of long-needed improvements in Ballybunion. At the present time it is difficult to make any appeal for funds, but we feel we are calling upon those who only are known to us personally by their presence year after year, and who have, very many of them, called our attention to evident drawbacks, and have urged us individually to take steps to bring Ballybunion into line with other popular watering places.

In appealing to our regular visitors we feel assured that we are appealing to our own. They are all well known to us and for the month or more are rather own fellow townspeople than strangers. This happy result would not be possible in the larger and more ambitious seaside places.

Those of you who come to Ballybunion and regard it as your regular summer resort are naturally interested in having conditions, outdoor as well as indoor, as comfortable as possible, and hence we are of the opinion that while the burden of the necessary improvements should in the main be borne by us, that you will not be indisposed towards co-operating in a project which would undoubtedly render your stay more pleasant and enjoyable.

Needless to say, you are aware that is not in our power to strike a local rate for the object we have in view, neither is it possible to raise the necessary funds by local subscriptions.

Natural Arch, Doon, 1890.

Main Street, Ballybunion, 1900s. (Image courtesy of William Lawrence Collection)

We hope to show by our contributions that we realise that the time has come to place Ballybunion in the front rank of popular seaside resorts.

Ballybunion has many natural advantages; its double strand is admirably for surf bathing. The Blackrocks, with a little expense, may afford excellent diving facilities both in open sea and in large pools.

Its cliffs are fortunately preserved by custom for the public. The sandhills afford a first-class Golf Course and very convenient walks. From the scenic point of view, Ballybunion leaves little to be desired. The new Wireless Station, in time, is sure to add to its importance and the larger the population, especially of a class who can live in comfort, the likelihood is there of many added advantages in the near future. The new Catholic church is an artistic gem and visiting priests will find that satisfactory arrangements are made for their convenience.

It is an earnest wish of the committee to expand to the best advantage the funds they can raise locally and from the visiting friends and to leave as little cause of complaint as possible in the future.

Any subscription will be gratefully received and acknowledged in due course.

Remain Yours Truly,
W. O'Carroll,
Hon. Secretary.

In the months and years to follow, the money was gathered and improvements were carried out by the committee. The Castle Green was renovated after the top was blown off in a storm and other sanitary issues along the strand were dealt with. This committee really left their mark on the town during those early years.

VISITORS TO BALLYBUNION, 1912

In 1912, Ballybunion was attracting visitors on a more regular basis. Local business people converted old houses into hotels, thus starting the hotel sector in the town, and these early boarding houses gave much-needed employment to the area. Many young local women obtained work during the summer months and there was much caretaking and grounds work for the men. Ballybunion was growing rapidly.

Hotels changed names and owners during this period of development and one such hotel was the Eagle Hotel (1886), which was owned by Mary E. Garvey. This hotel then became the

In this photo, dated 1912, a happy group is assembled outside the bar in Ballybunion. Sitting down with a falcon on his knee is Paddy Scanlon; the woman with a striped blouse was his mother (née Enright from the Exchange). Standing fifth in the back row with parted black hair is Maggie Dore (Kathleen's aunt), who worked there. In the centre of the three in front of window is Maggie Daly, who also worked there, and the distinguished man with the hat was the late Mike Power, Manager of the East End Creamery.

Ocean Hotel and later, when Aunt Kathy (Liston) from Athea married Paddy Scanlon in 1914, the name changed to O'Scanlain, a name chosen to defy the Black and Tans.

HEROES OF THE WAR OF INDEPENDENCE

Patrick Shortis, 1916

Patrick Shortis was one of the sons of William Shortis of Ballybunion. He was born on 4 July 1892. Patrick Shortis studied in Killarney and after receiving an excellent education he spent many years as a civil servant in London. Patrick became active in the Volunteer movement and in 1916 he fought for Irish freedom in the GPO, Dublin.

On Friday night of Easter Week, 1916, Patrick Shortis joined the assault on the barricade at Moore Street. He was shot by English forces and died next to his friend The O'Rahilly of Ballylongford.

A plaque on the front wall of the Bunker Bar in Ballybunion marks the birthplace of Patrick Shortis, a well known and respected member of the town's community.

The Shortis home.

Patrick Shortis, 1916.

Daniel Scanlon

Daniel Scanlon was a native of Ballybunion and came from a family that is to this day well known in the town. On 11 July 1917, a group of Irish Volunteers paraded through the town of Ballybunion. It has been stated that in the barracks at the time was a sergeant called Thorny Wire, who gave orders to shut up the windows of the barracks. This action caused a stir among the Volunteers. As they passed the barracks, stones were thrown and the group paraded on through the town to the Castle Green, where orations were being said.

When the assembly was over, the Volunteers matched back up the street in formation in the direction of the barracks. A shot was fired from the upper window and the crowd dispersed in all directions. However, Daniel Scanlon, a young man, lay dying on the street just across from the barracks, where it is said a fountain was sited. He was brought down the street to where a pub would later bear his name and died of his wounds there.

A plaque was place on the barracks many years later but a new monument was constructed and is located just at the side of Killcooley's Bar.

The O'Rahilly, 1916

In the quiet tranquil setting of Lisslaghtin Abbey, Ballylongford, amidst the birds singing in the rustling trees, stands a lone Celtic High Cross, which marks the spot where one of North Kerry's 1916 heroes lies – The O'Rahilly.

In that famous week in 1916, Ballybunion, Ballylongford and Ballyduff lost three of their sons on Moore Street: Patrick Shortis from Ballybunion, Michael Mulvihill from Ballyduff and The O'Rahilly from Ballylongford. In the decades since their deaths, they have not been forgotten, nor has what they did for Irish freedom.

Daniel Scanlon

Daniel Scanlon Monument, Main Street,
Ballybunion.

Michael Joseph O'Rahilly was born in Ballylongford in 1875 to a family who had built up a successful business. He was educated at University College Dublin and Clongowes College (1890-1892). He was a great believer in Irish nationalism and followed Arthur Griffith and the great leaders of the time by joining Sinn Féin. The O'Rahilly was the manager of *An Claidheamh Soluis*, which published an article by Eoin O'Neill that led to the establishment of the Irish Volunteers. The O'Rahilly had a vision for the movement, believing that one day Óglaigh Na hÉireann would be the legitimate defence force in the country.

In 1909, while on a business and a fundraising trip to America, The O'Rahilly met, and later married, Nannie Brown, the daughter of a rich socialite. In 1911, The O'Rahilly was one of the leaders of a group who tried to halt the visit of King George V to Dublin. Romantic and charismatic, he was also to be a key figure in the events that unfolded on the streets of Dublin in Easter Week, 1916.

The O'Rahilly was not in favour of a blood conflict and tried tirelessly to stop the rising after O'Neill's orders to halt the military operations were issued that week. In fact, The O'Rahilly drove around the countryside trying to stop the operation, but in the end it was too late. Instead of walking away, the Kerryman left his home and drove half the night to get to the GPO. When he got there he looked around. As he viewed the unfolding gun battle around him, he uttered the famous words, 'I have helped to wind the clock, now I have come to hear it strike.'

The battle that day was fierce; exchanges in fire with British troops were relentless. The

O'Rahilly, along with Patrick Shortis and Michael Mulvihill, defended the barricade near the GPO. Each man stood firm in the face of the consistent hail of fire from the English guns. During the barrage, The O'Rahilly, Shortis and Mulvihill took steps to drive forward up Moore Street. The O'Rahilly got trapped in a doorway by British snipers. He quickly made a run for cover but was shot and wounded; his two fellow Kerrymen, Shortis and Mulvihill, lay dead on the street a short distance away.

The O'Rahilly's wounds were to prove fatal. As his life ebbed away, he took a letter from his pocket and wrote, with his own blood, a final farewell to his beloved wife and family. In true Kerryman form, he wrote with his blood on a door near the spot

The O'Rahilly's Cross.

Jack Houlihan's War of Independence medal.

where he would eventually die, 'Here died The O'Rahilly RIP. On 28 April 1916, slumped in a doorway off Moore Lane, the Greatest Kerryman and Nationalist, The O'Rahilly died.'

The body of The O'Rahilly was later brought to a Dublin morgue, where it was said the famous note written in his blood was uncovered and forwarded to his family. Days later, the body of The O'Rahilly was brought back to Kerry and, in a ceremony befitting a hero, was laid to rest by his native Ballylongford people at the local cemetery of Lisslaghtin Abbey, a place shrouded with ancient Irish history.

In the days and months after the Rising, the streets around the GPO were in ruins. A large clean-up operation was under way, and heaps of rubble and twisted iron from the barricade at the GPO were transported to Croke Park for the building of Hill 16. Among the debris was a badly wrecked motor car. This was the car owned by The O'Rahilly, which he drove for the last time on that fateful day.

In the words of The O'Rahilly, 'It is madness, but it's glorious madness.'

MARCONI RADIO STATION, 1912-1924

In 1912, a site on Sandhill Road was purchased by the Marconi Radio Company from the local landlord George Hewson. This site consisted of seventy-two acres and was chosen because of its clear site line to the USA. No mountains would block the signal from the proposed radio station.

Humphrey's Steel Erecting Ltd of London were the contractors for the building process and up to 110 people worked on the station's construction. The workforce was all paid in gold sovereigns, a fact which to this day is still remembered. The materials for construction were transported by mainline rail to Listowel, then transported on the Lartigue Monorail and brought nine miles to Ballybunion. Then they were transported to the radio station by horse and cart.

The mast formation of the radio station was of umbrella design, consisting of a central mast of 500ft in height. It is stated locally that on the night the high mast was finished, a wind caught the guy ropes and pulled them from their housings, causing the mast to fall. The sound of the crashing mast was heard for miles distant. The second time the mast was erected, over eighteen tons of concrete were used for the central mast base and fifteen tons for the smaller bases.

A large petrol motor was constructed by Jose Fernando Company, Italy, and had to partly be housed underground. The purpose was to drive an electric generator which applied approximately 2.5 kilowatts at 12,000 volts to the oscillating valves, two of which were constructed by the Marconi Radio Company and were known as MTI. Two valves were used to power the oscillation generators.

In 1914, the Marconi Radio Station was ready and operating. The station operated during the First World War by the Royal Navy, with the telephony transmitter installed imputing 2.5kw. The station engineer W.T. Ditchem's voice crossed the Atlantic, and 3,800m later was received at Cape Breton, Nova Scotia.

The station house was constructed of pine and hosted the transmitter that was used by the engineers the day they transmitted across the Atlantic. It burned down many years ago. The Irish College is now built on the site. Today, nothing remains of the original station, only a commemorative stone and artefacts such as insulator wires and earth wires, which are in the safekeeping of the author.

Special thanks are due to John J. O'Carroll, who helped me compile this piece, look for artefacts and understand this valuable part of our local history.

Marconi Radio Station.

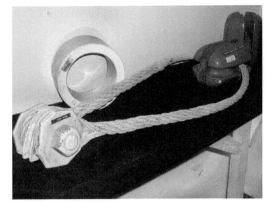

Above: *Marconi stay wire and insulators.*

Right: *The gate of Marconi Radio Station.*

Marconi Stone.

THE *PRINCESS XENIA* LANDS AT BEALE, 1927

On a cloudy Saturday afternoon on 16 September 1927 the sky over Beale echoed to the sound of a single-propeller aeroplane. This plane was piloted by R.M. Macintosh and co-piloted by Commandant James C. Fitzmaurice. Their mission was to cross the Atlantic to America from the military base at Baldonnel, County Dublin. However, the flight was disrupted due to changing weather conditions and the *Princess Xenia* was forced to turn back.

It has been said that the sound of the engine was heard for miles around, as the pilots attempted the landing, which they achieved on the strand at Beale. People came from far and wide to see the large, single-propeller airplane. The *Princess Xenia* was then moved with help of locals up to the shoreline, away from the coming tide.

Ballybunion man Paddy O'Sullivan afforded the crew his hospitality and drove them both to Ballybunion in his car, which famously had the nickname 'The Lizzy'. The crew stayed at the Central Hotel that night and were given a most warm welcome. When leaving, the pilots left a note thanking Paddy O'Sullivan for his hospitality.

On arriving at the plane on Sunday 17 September, R.M. Macintosh and Commandant James C. Fitzmaurice carried out their flight checks on the *Princess Xenia*. With the plane's single-propeller engine at full, the *Princess Xenia* taxied along the strand at Beale and took off into the sky to Baldonnel. Another attempt to cross the Atlantic was later made by the crew.

The Princess Xenia, Beale Strand, 1927. (Courtesy of P. O'Sullivan)

BALLYBUNION CONVENT SCHOOL, 1931

The old Ballybunion Convent School was located on Doon Road, where the present primary school is now situated. This building had high windows and a large entrance. The interior of the convent was, according to locals, just adequate. The school was run by the Sisters of Mercy, who had been in the area since the arrival of Mary O'Malley Young. A convent was located at the rear of the school in the former residence of Mary O'Malley Young. Due to its bad state of repair, the school was knocked down in the 1970s to make way for the new school.

Ballybunion Convent School, 1931. This rare photograph was taken of sixth and seventh class in 1931 near the rockery at the rear of the school. Back row: Maggie Keane, Peggie Holly, Lizzie Keane, -?-, Elis Bowen, Sheila Keane, Kathleen Handrahan, Mary McMahon, Marty Horgan, -?-, -?-, -?-, Lizzie Enright, Cathleen Brown, Mary Boyle. Third row: Brid Walsh, Nora Dalton, Lizzie Hannon, Mary Lynch, Cathy Ferris, Sheila Buckley, Eileen Neville, Marie Nagle, Pat O'Carroll, -?-, Nancy Foley, Connie Allen. Front Row: -?-, Maureen Walsh, Maureen O'Connor, -?-, Cissie Allen.

Old School Ballybunion, c. 1890.

Old School House, 1900s.

1932 OLYMPICS AND THE BALLYBUNION CONNECTION

In the annals of Irish sporting history, one event stands out for the year 1932: the Los Angeles Olympics. The event saw dreams realised and dreams dashed, but for Ireland the air was filled with celebration. Within ten minutes of the games commencing, two gold Olympic medals were won by Irish athletes – the first by Bob Tisdall, who won the 400 metre hurdles and the second by Dr Pat O'Callaghan, who won the hammer final with a throw of 176ft 11½in.

The Ballybunion Connection

In 1932, with the Los Angeles games fast approaching, Ballybunion was identified by Eamon Fitzgerald or General Owen O'Duffy (the then President of the Irish Olympic Council) as a suitable final training ground for the Irish track and field team. They would commence training on the world's finest set of sand dunes, now known as Ballybunion Golf Club's old course. The team of four were Bob Tisdall, Dr Pat O'Callaghan, Michael Murphy and Eamon Fitzgerald. The scene was set and within weeks was observed by all the locals of Ballybunion. The team quickly set up their training camp on the old eighteenth fairway (now the fifth fairway); the white hurdles contrasted with the green grass of the golf course. Within minutes, Tisdall, O'Callaghan and the team were training hard, up and down the long mown fairway. Their work seemed relentless.

It has been said that when asked about Ballybunion's training grounds, Bob Tisdall stated that 'the springiness of the turf added substantially to my speed'. Dr Pat O'Callaghan said, 'the area was the ideal spot, calm and peaceful'.

Apparently, the then-famous Kerry Senior Football Team trained on a number of occasions with Bob Stack on the course with the Olympic Team. Later that year they went on to win the All-Ireland.

After the Olympics, Bob Tisdall took up the game of golf and later became secretary of a golf course in Southampton, England. By the time the Olympic flame went down slowly in that Los Angeles night of 1932, Ballybunion was famous; not just for its fine scenery and golf, but as a destination for health and fitness.

CANON MICHAEL FULLER

On 29 October 1936, Canon Michael Fuller died. Canon Fuller was the parish priest of Ballybunion, and was a well-known and respected member of the community.

The Canon took a great interest in the town and its development from the 1900s onwards and supported the various drives to enhance the town's recognition as one of Ireland's best-known seaside resorts. He paid for considerable work in St John's church, such as on finishing altar rails and stained-glass windows.

When the news of the death of the Canon reached the town, there was a large outpouring of grief. In fact, the parish was in shock for days. Prior to his remains being brought to church, his heavy lead coffin was shouldered around the town by grieving parishioners who expressed their admiration for the late Canon.

Canon Fuller's funeral.

Canon Michael Fuller's tomb after the damage inflicted by vandals.

When the cortège passed Hennessey's and Shannon View on Main Street, the air was sombre; the crowd following the coffin with his cloak and hat grew to well in excess of a thousand. The coffin was brought to St John's church, where Requiem Mass was said, and then the remains of Canon Michael Fuller were laid to rest within the confines of the church. Ballybunion had lost a great friend and a good priest.

During the summer of 2010, the monument to the late Canon Fuller was damaged by vandals. There was local outrage and within days local people restored the tomb to its original condition. The Canon was buried in 1936, but his legacy prevails in the town of Ballybunion.

THE MINES OF THE SECOND WORLD WAR

During the war years in the 1940s, two mines were washed up in the Ballybunion area. One mine was beached near the Virgin's Rock, where the chimneys stood.

The late Martin Murphy and the late Sean Houlihan, then young boys, climbed down the cliffs and inspected one of the mines. The army had sandbagged the mine into a cave and a long wire was laid from the dynamite which led to the cliffs above, where the army and LDF were based. The youngsters were spotted in the cave and the army hurried them away to safety – indeed they saved their lives, said the late Sean Houlihan.

Right: *The LDF in the war years.*

Below: *Location of the Second World War mines found in Doon.*

The detonating charges were fired and the explosion could be heard for miles around. However, the force of the blast smashed the windows in the convent and knocked down the two sea stacks called the chimneys. Only the base of the chimneys stands today.

The second mine was found floating by the army near Tommy's Point on the Nun's Strand. This mine was scuttled by the army. In Doon a mine was found floating around Ri Na File. It was beached and the Gardaí and army evacuated the residents of Doon, from Leahys, Lynches, Griffins and Hunts to Robbie Stack's. This mine was blown up without damage to the area.

Mine enters Cuan Na Easic

A short time later in Doon, the army and LDF were alerted to another mine. This time the residents were not evacuated as the first time no damage was done to the locality. Ned Leahy's house was the nearest to the mine and according to the late Maryann Houlihan (*née* Leahy), she stayed with her father and the rest of the family went to Robbie Stack's. The army spent hours on the mine and then detonated it, and Maryann told the author that the window shuddered slightly as the mine was blown up.

Many weeks after the explosion, large pieces of the mine were collected by locals as mementos. In fact, a large piece of the mine was kept at Ned Leahy's forge for many years.

Second World War helmet and gas mask.

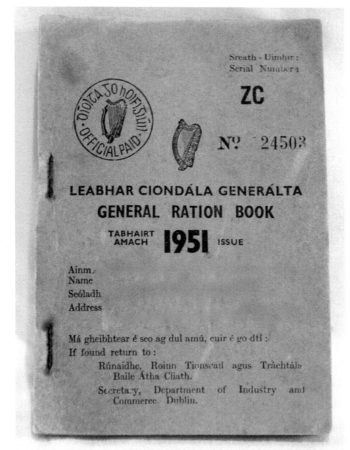

Ration Book, 1951.

BALLYBUNION PIPE BAND, 1948

The Ballybunion Pipe Band was founded by the late Dr Hannon and Fr Barry. This unique musical organisation formed part of the social community of the town of Ballybunion from 1948 to the late 1990s.

According to those who there at the time, the band has its roots at a GAA football final in Dublin, at which Dr Hannon and the late Jack Wash were present. Parading in front of the crowd was the Emerald Girls Pipe Band; it is said that Dr Hannon was very impressed, and after the match he approached them. Jack Walsh took a set of pipes in his hand and played them for the first time, and so he had the status of being the first piper from the Ballybunion Pipe Band to hold and play a set of bagpipes.

The Emerald Girls Pipe Band was not the first in the town; there was a band based within the Marconi radio station which had connections with the building of the golf club *c.* 1912. A chanter from this band existed in the town for many years.

Dr Hannon set about the formation of the band and within a short period of time practice had begun in Dr Hannon's cellar. The band started its life as a boy scouts' band and many photographs exist in which scout trousers are evident.

Ballybunion Pipe Band, c. 1950.

Carnival in Ballybunion, 1950s.

Instruction of the band

The first instructor of the pipe band was a man called Harnett from Listowel and with his help the band finally made its debut on the road (without any kilts or uniform). This town engagement was to have a more long-term effect on the band than otherwise thought. When the pipe band played the street that day for the first time, the town was in awe with the sound of the pipes, and so more people wanted to hear it and see it.

Subsequently, the band was requested to perform at parades, football matches and commemorations. It was during one such parade in the town of Ballybunion that the band made another connection, this time with the late Jimmy Fitzgerald of Main Street, Ballybunion, who would remain connected to the band until his death.

Jimmy Fitzgerald learned the bagpipes in Abbeyfeale in a place called Monagay under Pipe Major Michael Wall. Dr Hannon came down to Jimmy Fitzgerald's house and asked him to instruct the pipes; a long tradition in the town commenced on a proper musical footing.

The Pipes

Dr Hannon purchased all the instruments needed for the band – practice chanters, bagpipes, reeds, drums – and the original pipes were bought at Waltons in Dublin. These pieces served the band well for many years. The drums that were used in the band were tuned by tightening cords and were still in existence up until recently. The kilts were a McDonald tartan and the jackets were green with white belts and white spats. They were a well-turned-out band.

BALLYBUNION GREYHOUND RACING, 1935-1966

Ballybunion has, for many a dog breeder, an illustrious history of greatness and pedigree, with the founding and development of dog breeding, dog training and the history of the track and stadium.

In 1935, interest in greyhound racing was so great in the Ballybunion area that a company was founded called The Ballybunion Greyhound Racing Company Ltd. The board of directors included the late Charles Handrahan, honorary secretary, and the late James Clarke, director. The late William O'Carroll was another person who took a great interest in the development of greyhound racing and the development of the town of Ballybunion at that time.

The company, which was subject to the articles of association, lasted for many years and gave a good boost to the development of greyhound racing in the town of Ballybunion and in North Kerry in general. The share certificate was comprised of ordinary shares of 10s; the capital was £1,000 divided into 2,000 ordinary shares of 10s each. The company was incorporated under the Companies Acts of 1908-1917.

In the 1960s there was a revival of greyhound interest in the town. Locals began to train and to breed track dogs of high quality and one man, the late Matt O'Sullivan, pioneered an idea of a greyhound stadium purposely built within the town of Ballybunion, with all the modern facilities that a greyhound breeder would expect to find in anywhere in the world. In 1966, Matt O'Sullivan finished the work on one of Ireland's top greyhound racing stadia. This state-of-the-art facility was located on Sandhill Road.

Ballybunion Greyhound Racing Club.

Greyhound racing certificate, 1935.

Matt O'Sullivan. (Photo courtesy of the O'Sullivan family)

Directors and Officials

The main figures in Ballybunion greyhound racing at the time included: Matt O'Sullivan, chairman; Donal J. O'Neill, vice-chairman; Paddy O'Sullivan, Secretary; Brendan O'Sullivan, racing manager; James O'Rourke, MRCVS veterinary surgeon; Ken O'Sullivan, director; Ed Handrahan, director, and John Molyneaux, director. The late Dony Cooke of Doon Road also worked at the track for many years with Matt O'Sullivan.

On 18 May 1966 at 9 p.m., the blessing ceremony of the new greyhound stadium was performed by the Revd J.J. Murphy, parish priest. The official opening ceremony was performed by Bord Na gCon member Tom Fitzgibbon.

When the ceremonial tape cutting had ended, all dogs were placed in their traps for the first race, the Cashen Stakes (525 yards flat). The dogs were: trap 1 in red, *Cuba's Queen*; 2 in blue, *Kilflynn Boy*, 3 in white, *Queen Buffalo*; 4 in stripes, *Stand-In Lad*; 5 in black, *Remould Chieftain*; 6 in orange, *Spailpín Fánach*, and the reserve was *Humphrey's Gift*. The bell was sounded, the trapdoor released, and all dogs followed the hare towards the turn. Ballybunion had achieved the distinction of having its own greyhound stadium, which equalled the best in the world. All thanks to Matt O'Sullivan.

PRESIDENTIAL VISIT, 1940S

The town of Ballybunion has, for decades, hosted many visits from Presidents from around the world. The hospitality of the locals is known worldwide and with this the town has developed its 'céad míle fáilte' towards visiting dignitaries.

During the 1940s, one famous visitor caused a stir in the town: President Éamon De Valera, who was canvassing in the town during the election. Many locals came out to support the famous man and the event was the talking point in the town for weeks. Jim Clarke, a well-known Ballybunion man at that time, met with De Valera in the grounds of Clarke's Pub, now known as Killcooley's Bar. A long conversation on politics took place and many jokes and tales were told between the two men. The day was a great success for De Valera and for the residents of Ballybunion, who never forgot to give its visiting dignitaries a good Irish welcome.

Election time in Ballybunion. (Photo courtesy of the late Phillis Diggins)

SAVING THE HAY IN THE 1950S

Long hard days were spent working in the fields, saving the hay, during the 1940s and '50s. Prior to the arrival of modern mechanisation in the farmyards of North Kerry, all tasks were done by hand – some by labourers but most by the neighbours who would give a helping hand when the work on the family farm got busy.

When hay was being saved in the fields of Ballybunion and Beal, large crowds of friends and neighbours would gather. Hours were spent working with the two-prong and three-prong pikes and the hay was gathered into heaps. A hay car was used to bring the hay back to the barn to be used during the long winter.

Large earthenware bottles called porter jars or growlers were distributed in the fields after the day's hard work had ended. Everyone had a drink of porter and soon a song would be heard and then a dance would take place. This was the custom that has now sadly vanished.

When modern hay-saving machinery arrived, it meant the end of the days in the field with the neighbours; where once fields were filled with conversation and laughter, now there was the sound of one machine and its driver.

Right: *In this photograph, taken many years ago in a field now long forgotten in Ballybunion, are three local men who spent a hard and happy day saving the hay. Those friends were Timmy Lyons, Long Paddy and Mr Clarke.*

Below left: *Hay knife from Barnadarrig, 1960s.*

Below right: *Main Street, Ballybunion, 5 May 1957. (Photo courtesy of Michael Beasley)*

At the end of the year, when all the hay, turf and crops were gathered in, there farming communities in the Ballybunion and North Kerry areas held a celebration. The Annual Harvest Festival in Listowel and 15 August in Ballybunion were the focal points during the year, when everyone in the Ballybunion area who had worked hard on the land during the year came together. They discussed the year's outcome on the farm, matches were made and the next year was planned.

A PIONEER OUTING FROM THE PAST

One fine sunny day, a large group of Ballybunion pioneers assembled in front of Muckcross House in Killarney to celebrate the movement in Ballybunion. This was also a time to contemplate the vows taken and to connect with the spiritual side of life in Ireland at that time.

In 1898, the Pioneer Total Abstinence Association was founded in Dublin by Fr James Cullen. Its mission was Devotion to the Sacred Heart, with a spiritual thread that was to run through the movement down through the ages.

The organisation was controlled by a central council in Dublin and funds were initially raised by the selling of Pioneer pins and later an association magazine. Ballybunion had its own branch, which was constituted under the rules of the PTAA. At each meeting, the secretary read out the minutes and correspondence and this always finished with a prayer called 'The Heroic Offering'. Possible fundraisers and outings were also discussed during these meetings.

Ballybunion Pioneers.

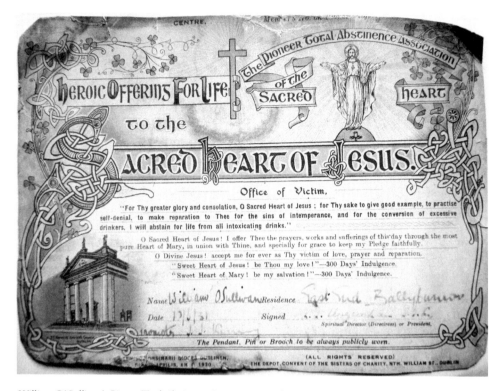

William O'Sullivan's Pioneer Total Abstinence Association Certificate, 1931.

In the 1940s and '50s, the movement had grown and so had the Ballybunion association, with Ballydonoghue being incorporated into the Ballybunion association's monthly meetings, which were then held at the home late William O'Sullivan on Church Road. William O'Sullivan was the President at that time and had joined the association at the age of twenty-three. Fr Barry, the local curate, would advise the gathering on all aspects of the proceedings. Also prominent at that time among the association were Jack O'Sullivan and Willie McCabe.

During the years of the Church Road meetings of the PTAA, one man travelled a round trip of ten miles on bad roads on his bicycle without fail from Beal. He was Eddie Creed. He is a shining example of the commitment of the locals in the Pioneer Association in Ballybunion.

FEALE AND CASHEN DRAINAGE SCHEME, 1951

During the 1950s the Feale and Cashen catchment area was flooding. The estuary had silted with mud clogging up to 5ft and the nearby farms were being severely damaged on a yearly basis, so a solution had to be found.

The Board of Works drafted a plan to relieve the area, first by contacting Erskine Childers, who asked his contacts in America to look out for a dredging machine. Childers was at that time the manager of Blackwood Hodge Ltd. The decision was made to use one of Europe's first portable suction dredgers, based at the mouth of the Cashen River, working inwards towards the ferry bridge. The massive dredger was sold to the Office of Public Works by Richard Wably, who was, at the time, the manager of Blackwood Hodge.

The Dredger, 22 January 1952

The dredger was shipped in box sections of forty tons to Dublin Port and transported to the banks of the Cashen River by trucks. It took six days to assemble the massive dredger, including painting. The work was supervised by dredger expert H. W. Buck, who worked for the Panama Company and trained the workers as they went along.

At last the dredger was completed and at half past five on the following Monday, the £22,000 Elliot Suction Dredger, with the help of a tractor, floated onto the river, with the large discharge

Above: *Sean Houlihan and Senan Conroy, Ballybunion.*

Right: *Levels being taken for the Cashen drainage scheme.*

pipes placed on floating pontoons. Immediately, Europe's first portable suction dredger went into action. As the large onboard engine started up under the supervision of the late Senan Conroy of Ballybunion and skipper Pat Daly from County Offaly, the problems of flooding were soon to be over for the area.

Cashen Drainage Specifications

The suction dredger had an 8in-diameter pump and a discharge pipe, discharging up to 100/150 cubic yards an hour. The depth of the Cashen River prior to the dredge was 5ft and after drainage it was 12ft deep and 80ft wide. The dredger on the River Cashen delivered 1,200 cubic yards in four days and could dredge in waters up of to 20ft deep or as shallow as 4ft. Along the river, four massive draglines were used to work on the embankments and back drains. These machines were very effective and proved very reliable. In the locality the drainage gave much-needed employment and indeed the training and experience led others to further work prospects.

In 1951, a Ruston-Bucyrus dragline of sixteen tons arrived on the Cashen Drainage Scheme. This machine, which was converted from steam to petrol and finally to diesel, had a 50hp Dorman engine and would prove very reliable. The cab was constructed with a felted roof and had three windows, one door and one half door. The dragline had a half-yard bucket at the time. This machine was thirty-two years old when it arrived at the Cashen.

Immediately the combination of the river suction dredger and the four draglines were having an effect; large embankments rose along the River Cashen and the back drains and slew gates opened and closed as the tidal waters ebbed and flowed.

The Ruston-Bucyrus worked its way up the river to Horgans of Meevuc and then to Ballyegan, and according to the dragline operators the machine gave little trouble compared the newer ones.

In Ahabeg Lixnaw, the Board of Works operators were Paddy Mannix, banksman, Abbeydorney and Mick Sheehy (RIP), ganger, and from Athamore Causeway to Bally McQuinn Castle there was Sean Houlihan, machine operator, Paddy Costello, ganger, and Michael Scanlon, banksman.

The late Sean Houlihan of Ballybunion, who was the Ruston-Bucyrus operator at that time, told the author that the workers on the Cashen Drainage started at eight in the morning and finished at six. There was a break at ten in the morning for a quarter of an hour (which wasn't strictly allowed but did take place).

In the canal leading to Bally McQuinn Castle, a bed of solid rock was uncovered. The team ordered two Broomwade compressors from the Board of Works yard, which were pulled to the site by tractors. Owen Horgan of Lixnaw was the operator of one of them. Large holes for the gelignite were drilled in the rock by Owen; then the Guards were called and the gelignite was laid and fired by Mick Gilmore, section foreman of the Board of Works.

In the year 2010, a large bank of sand that was removed in 1952 returned and flood took place in the area once more. The marks of the draglines have been seen from time to time in the mud – reminders of what was done in the past and what will have to be done again in the future on the Cashen River.

THE AHAFONA MARIAN GROTTO, 1954

Marian Grottos were erected throughout the Irish countryside during 1954 on instruction from the Vatican under Pope Pius XII, who dedicated 1954 the Marian Year in honor of Mary. During that year, hundreds of people visited holy places and joined Holy Orders; it was a year of reflection and prayer.

The shrines and grottos like Ahafona were constructed to specifications laid down by the Church in Rome. Communities like Ballybunion undertook and completed the request to erect an altar in which the image of the Blessed Virgin was enshrined.

Marian Grotto, Ahafona.

The Ahafona Grotto was opened on a very wet day on 1954 with hundreds in attendance. It was a new place where the community could stop for a while, pray and reflect. To this day in the Ahafona area, the local community has a deep respect for the grotto and future generation owe a debt of gratitude to the people of the area who worked to construct it.

Michael Miley Cooke, a well-known native of Ahafona, has been very busy for the last twenty-seven years, keeping the grotto clean, painting and cutting hedges. Miley's late wife Doreen Cooke loved the grotto and spent many hours there looking after it, and so Miley has dedicated all his work on the grotto to the memory of his late wife and the community of Ballybunion.

The grotto is located at the junction at Ahafona and is visited by hundreds of visitors on a yearly basis. It is well worth a visit for a quiet prayer.

BALLYBUNION'S MOST FAMOUS DANCER AND SINGER

On 25 January 1983, one of Ballybunion's most famous residents was laid to rest in Listowel Cemetery: Jack Lyons of Belmount Church Road.

In the eyes of many, Jack Lyons was one of the country's most loved and respected musicians; a concertina player and a dancer of high stature who performed at Fleadhanna Cheoil and winner of many All-Ireland and local medals for his talents.

The countryside of North Kerry was saddened by the passing of Jack Lyons on that January day of 1983 and his family and friends in Ceoilthas Ceoiltóirí Éireann reflected on the man who everyone called their friend. His collection of old Irish songs was vast and his favourite reel, 'The Eel in the Sink', was one of his own compositions.

Jack Lyons travelled the countryside of Ireland for a session; whether at a wake or a funeral he always left the crowd assembled in awe and in laughter with his stories of bygone Ireland. In Ballybunion, Jack was known to sing and dance at his local pub, which was the centre of the community in the 1960s. There, among the crowds of both young and old, a happy man displayed his talents to an always appreciative audience.

On 23 January 1983, Jack Lyons of Belmount Church Road, Ballybunion, passed away, leaving behind him a legacy of music, song and dance.

LOCAL HISTORIAN MATTY LEAHY, BROMORE

Born in Bromore, Matty Leahy was a well-known local whose life touched many in the countryside of Doon and beyond. Matty was a kind-hearted person who loved nature, local history and folklore.

Matty Leahy grew up in a house in Bromore adjacent to the Leahy forge. The house was full of stories, and heritage passed down from generation to generation from his grandmother Biddy Leahy (née Walsh). Biddy Leahy was well known as a midwife and a woman who was good at treating ailments. She also prepared people on their way to the hereafter.

One particular story of Matty's involved the hunter and his dog. The story relates that a hunter and his dog pursued a rabbit near a ring fort in a field called Pairc Quirke, crossing the hedges and ditches until the rabbit was caught in the shade of a ditch and bitten by the dog. Injured, the rabbit made its way into a nearby thatched house.

When the hunter and the dog approached the house and asked if a rabbit had entered, the owner of the thatched house replied no. The hunter thanked him and just as he was walking away, he noticed the old man by the fire with blood dripping from his hand.

Matty related to the author that according to the myth, the old man could change into a rabbit due to an ancient enchantment and by evening could change back to an old man. These were the kind of stories told around the old fireplace in Bromore, when the day's long hard toil in the family forge was over. Before Matty would speak a word, the pipe was filled with Old Holborn and then, with a cup of strong tea, the stories were told.

Many a long fine day Matty strolled along the cliffs from Lick Castle to his cousin's house at Doon. There he would get all the news from the forge at Doon, and when his cousin Dan Joe was there, he used his telescope to view the cliffs and wildlife of the haggards and Ri Na File.

Sadly Matty Leahy passed away in the late 1990s and with him a great history of the area was lost. Thankfully Matty passed on a considerable number of myths and legends to the author, so continuing the art of folklore in the area.

Historian Matty Leahy on Doon Point, 1950s.

O'CARROLL'S SHOP

Ballybunion: An Illustrated History would not be complete without a mention of one of its most famous buildings, O'Carroll's. Located on the Main Street, this shop was founded by the O'Carroll family at the end of the 1700s and became famous for its hospitality and friendship to all who entered its doors. In fact, the family gave much-needed employment in the area down through the decades, from its foundation as a shop to its later Lounge Bar. The shop was run by the O'Carrolls and, in the history of the shop, both William and Patrick O'Carroll played their parts in the development of the business and the town.

O'Carroll's shop was the forerunner to the modern-day supermarket; in its heyday O'Carroll's was well stocked with normal day-to-day items and imported, more unusual articles. O'Carroll's always made the customer happy, thus the trade was built up over the decades. The shop had a mill at the rear and had a small bottling facility to bottle porter in those early days.

The family were well respected and liked in the town of Ballybunion due to their interest in the development of the town as a family seaside resort at the dawn of the 1900s. The family was also instrumental in advising the tenants in the purchase of their holdings from the landlord George Hewson.

O'Carroll's Shop, 1884.

In the annals and old faded books of the shop, we read that on 10 January 1834, Fr Mortimer O'Connor, parish priest, paid for five gallons of oil at the cost of 4s 2d. On 15 September, Mr George Hewson, the local landlord, visited the shop and obtained a pike and oil totalling 7s for his Ennismore estate. O'Carroll's also had an account active with the military; on a daily basis the constabulary mess obtained one pound of tea, a quarter of sugar, three pounds of soap and three pounds bread, which cost 1s 3d. The Marconi Radio Company, which had an account in the shop, had fruit, whiskey and other daily items brought to the station from the time of its construction to the transmission date in 1919.

During the war years, O'Carroll's managed to stay well stocked. In 1943, preserves were obtained from R. & W. Scott Ireland Ltd, with jars of strawberry jam costing 12s per dozen. Biscuits were obtained from W. & R. Jacob & Co. Ltd, Dublin, on 1 May 1944 at the cost of £2 11s for eighteen tins and two boxes. E. Smithwick & Sons Ltd provided Brew 57, 1 Kiln No.1 Ale at £4 15s. For the housewife of the time, one of the most important items stocked in the shop was tea. This was obtained from Newsom & Sons Ltd, Cork, importers of Assam, Indian, and Chinese teas.

The shop continued to operate successfully in the town throughout the 1950s and 1960s. Later it was renovated and converted to a Lounge Bar by one of the descendents, John Higginbotham, who ensured that the good service and hospitality for which the building was renowned was continued. Sadly the doors of this once-famous building were closed in the early years of the twenty-first century, and so closed an important chapter in Ballybunion's history.

Viva Petty (née) O'Carroll.

O'Carroll's today.

SUNDAY'S WELL

Sunday's Well, or Tobar Ri An Domnaigh, was located on the Glen Road. It was a place venerated by all who visited it. People who had eye problems or illnesses believed that wells like this would give them cures. This well, according to locals, was a clear spring well which was used by many for water for their homes.

Pattern Day was 15 August and the day became associated with Sunday's Well due to the large numbers of people visiting Ballybunion after devotion at the local churches at Doon and St John's. Religious stalls selling rosary beads ran a good trade during Pattern Days in the area.

Many stories have been told about the well, including one of a holy trout that was seen in the well. It was said the sight of the magical trout could cure illness. It was said that Sunday's Well was once on the opposite side of the road (on the left-hand side going down to the ladies' beach). One day a visiting woman washed her clothes in it and the next day the well had dried up and moved itself to the right-hand side of the road.

In Ireland at that time the annual Pattern Day was a day not just for prayers and visiting wells like Sunday's Well, but one of fun and trouble. Large quantities of alcohol were consumed in the towns and villages and fights often broke out.

Over time, Patterns like that at Sunday's Well in Ballybunion died out and the religious connections were lost. It was during this period that Sunday's Well fell into a bad state of repair; it was vandalised a few times and then the cliff scaled in on it. Finally the council covered the well for safety reasons. Today nothing remains, but water from the well still flows out from its original location.

BLACKSMITH OF DOON

The forge at Doon was located just beyond the creamery on the left-hand side of the road. It was established by the late Ned Leahy, whose father, John Leahy, operated a forge in Bromore. Ned Leahy learned his trade of blacksmith and farrier at the Leahy's forge in Kilrush, County Clare. It was there he learned the art of turning and shaping steel and the care of horses, and it was also there that he met his future wife, Christina Grogan. The family moved to Lixnaw first, where there was a forge at Leahy's at Clandouglas Cross. There the first of his children, Mary Ann, was born. Later Ned moved to Ballybunion to construct a forge.

Ned was first offered a site on Church Road, but thought that a forge in the countryside might prove better as it would be close to the farming community. A site was found just beyond Doon church, which was owned by a Carrig man and later Ned built his house, with the forge at the bottom of the garden. Ned and Christina had three children there: Dan Joe (Danjo), Eamon and Theresa.

Blacksmith's anvil, Doon forge.

Ned Leahy's two sons, Danjo and Eamon, attended Killconly School under the late Garret Pierce, and the two daughters, Mary Ann and Theresa, attended the convent school in Ballybunion.

The forge quickly became established in the locality, with horses and carts tied up along the road in the direction of Robbie Stack's. Ned attended to all the needs of the farmers of Doon, Beale, Bromore, Asdee and beyond, their horses and ironwork. It was a hard life but he liked his work and walked the short distance to his house from the forge at the bottom of the garden each day.

In Doon, Ned produced horseshoes and donkey shoes and he manufactured implements such pot hooks for fireplaces and very ornate turned ironwork, such as that used in the doors of St John's church, Ballybunion, which can be still seen to this day.

The forge in Bromore was at that time still in operation and Ned would alternate between the two. It was at Bromore that the bands were prepared and placed on the wooden wheels for banding. The iron was heated in the fire and lifted by drags or dogs by Ned and his brother Michael Leahy to the large stone outside, where the wooden cartwheel was ready. Here the new band was placed on the wooden wheel and heavy sledge work commenced, often by moonlight. When the sledge work was finished, water from the well near the forge was poured on the wheel, finishing the process.

The forge at Doon was equipped with all the tools a blacksmith and farrier needed: two anvils, farrier's stand, two top and bottom fullers, top and bottom swages, hot-set or hot-centre punches, cold set, Stamp, pincers and pritchel. Some of the larger tools that Ned used in the Doon and Bromore forges were: three large tongs, a scroll dog, 7lb sledge, a hoof-pairing knife, small and large mandrills, a cat's-head hammer used for making horseshoes, a shoeing hammer,

One of Ned Leahy's forge tools.

Theresa, Christina and Mary Ann Leahy.

St John's church door.

and buffers for knocking off clenches. The forge had a large, hand-operated wooden bellows, which was manually operated by Ned Leahy to blow the hot coal forge fire on a daily basis.

The forge at Doon was focal point, where Ned read the newspaper every day to all who had arrived with their horses. A lively debate would always be on the cards at Ned's forge; during the war years the advance of Hitler's army was monitored and discussed as the shoes went on the horses and the ironwork was beat and shaped on the anvil.

The view of the Shannon estuary from the door of the forge was extensive. The countryside was rich and green in colour, and during the war years the LDF could be heard making their way back to the hut and on the road to the island behind the forge to attend to the mines that had been washed in near Ri Na File.

At one stage, Ned worked in the blacksmiths' forge in Bord Na Mona, fixing and mending the large machines which the company put on the bogs.

The Forge at Doon closed during the late 1960s when Ned Leahy retired. The age of the blacksmith of Doon was over. Ned Leahy died on 8 December 1976 aged seventy-five and was buried in Killehenny Cemetery with his father Jack, mother Brigit Leahy (*née* Walsh) and his son Danjo. Ned's daughter Mary Ann Houlihan is buried in a grave next to the Leahy grave.

> My sledge and anvil lie declined,
> My bellows too have lost their wind
> My fires extinct, my forge decayed,
> And in the dust my vice is laid,
> My coal is spent, my irons gone,
> My nails are drove, my work is done.

(Epitaph to William Strange, blacksmith, who died June 1746)

THE CENTRAL BALLROOM

The official opening of the Central Ballroom, Ballybunion took place on Sunday 29 June 1956. *The Kerryman* reported the opening event in style, estimating that 10,000 people had turned up to hear the Roxburghs Band play.

The late Matt O'Sullivan's ballroom was in full motion, with patrons filling the hall to hear the band and enjoy the night's festivities. The Central Ballroom was now a major nightspot for the people of North Kerry and beyond.

On 8 September 1956, the Maurice Mulcahy Band stepped onto the stage at the Central Ballroom and wooed the audience with their musical brilliance. This band would appear regularly in the town from 1957 to the 1970s. The band was well liked in the locality and even one of its own, Jack Noonan, played in the band.

The group was founded by the late Maurice Mulcahy in 1951, along with his three brothers Dave, Michael and Joe. In its early years, the band played in Micheltown and other towns in their area. The music they played was known far and wide, their repertoire featuring the best of Glenn

Matt O'Sullivan, owner of the Central Ballroom.

The Maurice Mulcahy Band.

The Central Ballroom microphone.

BALLYBUNION

The new sensation in Dance Music

Maurice Mulcahy

AND HIS BAND

NOW RECKONED AS ONE OF IRELAND'S BEST

will make its first appearance at the new

CENTRAL BALLROOM

Saturday and Sunday nights next

(SEPTEMBER 8th AND 9th)

FIRST APPEARANCE ALSO AT THE BALLROOM

Wednesday night, Sept. 12th

OF

Johnny McMahon

AND HIS ORCHESTRA

Direct from very successful season at the Hydro Hotel, Kilkee.

Dancing each night at 9 p.m.   ::   Popular Prices.

GUEST ARTIST — MISS MOLLIE MILLAR

You must enjoy yourself at the Central Ballroom !

Poster advertising 'new sensation' Maurice Mulcahy at the Central Ballroom, Ballybunion.

The Central Ballroom.

Bunny Dalton and his band.

McLeod's Ballroom.

Atlantic View House.

Miller and all the dance bands. Quantity and quality were the hallmarks of the band's success. They went on stage at 9 p.m. six nights a week and played until 1 a.m.

During the 'Swinging Sixties', Ballybunion was in full motion; all dance halls were full and the Central was full to capacity on a nightly basis. Those were the nights of glamour, with women and men dancing the night away to the sounds of the Maurice Mulcahy Band and the greats of the era. The parish priest often preached about the evils of low light and soft music but of course this fell on the deaf ears of the young lovers of the dance hall age in Ballybunion.

References

1901 Census

Ainsworth, William, *The Caves of Ballybunion* (1834)

Ballybunion Golf Club archive file 3425

Ballybunion Greyhound Racing Program

Ballybunion Heritage and Historical Society file 17571 (1995)

Ballydonoghue Parish Magazine (2000)

Barrington, T.J., *Discovering Kerry*

Bishop Coffey's Report

Bourke, Edward J., *Shipwrecks of the Irish Coast 1105-1993*

Byrne, Mathew J., *Rattoo*

Carmody, Vincent, *North Kerry Camera 1860-1960*

Cashen Drainage, file 91324, Ballybunion Heritage Archive

Casserley, H., *The Listowel & Ballybunion Railway*

Clarke, Phil, interview Ballyeagh Faction Fight, 1834

Costello, Patsy, research 2010

Feehan, John M., *The Secret Places of The Shannon*

Feenhan, John M., *The Magic of the Coast of Kerry*

Flahive, Michael, *The Last Voyage of The Dronningen*

Gaughan, Fr Anthony, *Listowel & Its Vicinity*

Griffith's Valuation (1852)

Guerin, Michael, *The Lartigue Listowel & Ballybunion Railway*

Hayward, Richard, *In the Kingdom of Kerry*

Houlihan, Danny, *Ballybunion and its Railway History*

Houlihan, Danny, 'Ballybunion Historical Places of Interest' (1991)

Houlihan, Danny, 'Doon church and its history' (1997)

Houlihan, Mary Ann, *Ghost Ships of the Shannon* (1998)

Houlihan, Mary Ann, *River Boats of the Shannon* (1991)

Kerry Archaelogical Society, *The Famine in Kerry* (1997)

King, *History of Kerry*

Lartigue, *William Shortis*

Limerick Harbour Commision Survey

Lysaght, Paddy, *The River Feale*

Marconi Radio Station, file 3967, Ballybunion Heritage Archive

Marian Shrine Ahafona, file 2210, Ballybunion Heritage Archive

McCarthy, Robert, *Trinity College Estates, 1800-1923*

Newham, A.T., *The Listowel & Ballybunion Railway*

O'Carroll's Shop Ledger (1834), Ballybunion Heritage Museum Archive

O'Ciosain, Michael, *Cnoc an Fhomhair*

O'Donnell, Patrick, *Irish Faction Fighters of the 19th Century*

O'Donovan, *The Annals of The Kingdom of Ireland by The Four Masters*

O'Kelly, Michael J., *Early Ireland*

O'Sullivan, Chairman Senator Ned, North Kerry Archaeological Survey

Ordnance Sureu. Listowel 1in sheets 150, 151

Quinlan, Sean, *The Great Book of Kerry Volume 3*

Redmond, John, *Ballybunion Golf Club: An Illustrated History 1893-1993*

Register of Baptisms in the Parish of Liselton in the County of Kerry and Diocese of Ardfert
    (1882).

Shore Dwellers, file 17570, Ballybunion Heritage Archive.

Smith, *History of Kerry*

Strand Magazine

Tarrant & O'Connell, 'North Kerry Archaelogical Survey

The Shannon Side Annual 1959

Times Pictorial (Week ending 1 March 1952)

Walsh, Jack, *Ballybunion Where I Live*

Warnet, Les, *Lartigue-Mallet and the Listowel & Ballybunion Mono Railway*